How to Improve Your Mind

Also by Andrew Wright

In this series:
How to Communicate Successfully
How to Enjoy Paintings
How to be Entertaining
How to be a Successful Traveller

with David Betteridge and Michael Buckby:
Games for Language Learning

with Michael Beaumont:
Teacher's Guide to the How to . . . readers

Pictures for Language Learning

with Penny Ur:
Five–Minute Activities

How to
Improve Your Mind

Andrew Wright

with drawings by the author

CAMBRIDGE
UNIVERSITY PRESS

Published by the Press Syndicate of the University of Cambridge
The Pitt Building, Trumpington Street, Cambridge CB2 1RP
40 West 20th Street, New York, NY 10011–4211, USA
10 Stamford Road, Oakleigh, Victoria 3166, Australia

© Cambridge University Press 1987

First published 1987
Third printing 1992

Printed and bound in Great Britain by
J. W. Arrowsmith Ltd, Bristol

ISBN 0 521 27550 4

SE

Contents

Contents

Thanks

I would like to thank Alison Silver, the editor of this series who has made a significant contribution to each book in terms of content and presentation. I would also like to thank Monica Vincent for her valuable advice, Peter Donovan for his support during the long period of writing and Peter Ducker for his concern for the design and typography. I am also grateful to the teachers and students of Nord Anglia for trying out samples of the texts and giving me useful advice for their improvement.

In a book of this kind one is naturally influenced by a large number of writers, lecturers, friends and acquaintances. However, I should like to acknowledge the following writers and their books in particular: J.M. and M.J. Cohen, *Modern Quotations*, Penguin; *The Oxford Dictionary of Quotations*, Oxford University Press; *The International Thesaurus of Quotations*, Penguin; Tony Busan, *Use Your Head*, BBC Publications; Edward de Bono, *Practical Thinking* and *Po: Beyond Yes or No*, Pelican; Alan Maley and Françoise Grellet, *Mind Matters*, Cambridge University Press; James Adams, *Conceptual Blockbusting*, W.W. Norton & Co. Inc.; Robert H. McKim, *Experiences in Visual Thinking*, Brooks/Cole Publishing Company; Alan Baddeley, *Your Memory*, Pelican; Gwen Ansell, *Make the Most of Your Memory*, National Extension College; C.H. Waddington, *Tools for Thought*, Paladin; Edith Rudinger (ed.) *Living With Stress*, Consumer Association; Manya and Eric de Leeuw, *Read Better, Read Faster*, Pelican; Michael Wallace, *Study Skills in English*, Cambridge University Press; Gerald Mosback and Vivienne Mosback, *Practical Faster Reading*, Cambridge University Press; Edward Fry, *Reading Faster*, Cambridge University Press.

I have also used one of my own stories from *Moments* (a collection of short stories) published by Pilgrims, Canterbury, 1986.

About this book

How to Improve Your Mind is one in a series of five books. There are five chapters, each dealing with a different aspect of improving your mind. There are several different sections in each chapter, and some will probably be more interesting and relevant to you than others. There is no need to read every section. I hope you will find it all interesting and entertaining, and that your reading of English will improve as well as your abilities.

★ Indicates that there is a question you should think about on your own.

★★ Indicates that if you are reading the book with another person you should talk about this particular question with him or her.

You may be reading the book while studying English in a class, with a teacher, or you may be reading it at home in the evenings, or on a train, or anywhere else – it doesn't matter!

What I do hope is that you enjoy reading about improving your mind – in English!

Some thoughts about thinking

★ Do you agree with any of them?

It isn't that they can't see the solution. It is that they can't see the problem.
(G.K. Chesterton (1874–1936), *The Point of a Pin*)

In my experience, the worst thing you can do to an important problem is discuss it.
(Simon Gray (b. 1936), *Otherwise Engaged*)

Only the educated are free.
(Epictetus, *Discourses*, 2nd C)

Education is the ability to listen to almost anything without losing your temper or your self-confidence.
(Robert Frost, *Reader's Digest*, 1960)

By nature all men are alike, but by education widely different.
(Chinese Proverb)

Children have to be educated, but they have also to be left to educate themselves.
(Ernest Dimnet, *The Art of Thinking*, 1928)

Knowledge is power.
(Francis Bacon, 'De Haeresibus', *Meditationes Sacrae*, 1597)

Information's pretty thin stuff, unless mixed with experience.
(Clarence Day, 'The Three Tigers,' *The Crow's Nest*, 1921)

The great difficulty in education is to get experience out of ideas.
(George Santayana, *The Life of Reason: Reason in Common Sense*, 1905–6)

We distrust our heart too much, and we don't distrust our head enough.
(Joseph Roux, *Meditations of a Parish Priest*, 1886)

To be able to enjoy one's past life is to live twice.
(Martial, *Epigrams*, 86 AD)

A great memory does not make a philosopher, any more than a dictionary can be called a grammar.
(John Henry Newman, *The Idea of a University*, 1853–8)

'*She reads at such a pace,' she
complained, 'and when I asked
her where she had learnt to read
so quickly she replied "On the
screens at cinemas."'*
(Ronald Firbank, *The Flower Beneath
the Foot*, 1923)

*I took a course in speed reading,
learning to read straight down
the middle of the page, and was
able to read* War and Peace *in
twenty minutes. It's about
Russia.*
(Woody Allen, quoted in Peter and
Josie Holton, *Quote and Unquote*)

Our wonderful brain

We can't improve our intelligence but we can improve the ways in which we use it. Our brain is wonderful and yet it is difficult for our brain to realise how wonderful it is!

The brain weighs about 1.5 kg and contains between ten and fifty thousand million neurones. In one part of the brain (the cerebellum) there are as many as sixty thousand connections (synapses) for each neurone! The brain still makes the biggest computer seem clumsy in most ways.

But do we use this wonderful possession as well as possible? Certainly not. We seem unable to get away from our limited and traditional ways of thinking. Thinking is not just a reflection of our brain but a skill – a skill which needs time and practice to develop. Gradually it becomes 'natural' and other people may assume that we were born with the skill and that we are very lucky.

Most animals know how to relax and they 'know' the importance of relaxation to their survival. Energy has to be saved for when it is needed and must not be wasted on tension and excitement. A basic skill for our own survival in this competitive world is the skill of relaxation: the next chapter makes a few suggestions which might contribute to the building of this skill.

There are a number of thinking skills. A most important skill is knowing how to make use of our natural creativity, and some ideas for developing this are described in the following chapter. The ability to find information rapidly is important in this 'age of information', and there are some ideas in the following chapter for developing the ability to remember. In the last chapter the skill of reading quickly is described and suggestions are made for its development.

It demands involvement to develop a physical or a mental skill. We can't just read about how to play tennis or how to paint, we have to try to do them. Each section of this book demands involvement too, and there are various suggestions for your active involvement. It is only by trying the suggestions that you can find out whether or not you can 'improve your mind'!

BRAIN! YOU ARE WONDERFUL!

How to reduce stress and tension

Modern life in the Western world is stressful. We compete at work and often in sport and even with our friends. We try to save time and try to earn as much money as possible in order to possess cars, better houses, washing machines or to go on holiday so that we can relax after becoming so tense and tired!

Stress

What makes you stressed?

2

Signs of stress

★ Have you noticed any of these signs in yourself or in another person recently? Are these signs increasing?

- irritability
- fussiness
- gloominess
- suspicion
- indecision
- excitability
- restlessness
- lack of concentration
- unsociability
- loss of appetite
- over-eating
- sleeplessness
- drinking
- smoking
- worrying
- tension

What is causing the stress?

Many people try to get rid of the signs of stress instead of the cause. They may take sleeping pills or try to control the various signs in other ways. But the only satisfactory way of stopping stress is to find the cause of it. You may not be able to change the cause of the stress but understanding it will probably help.

It may be the death or illness of a friend, the loss of your job or money worries. And you can probably do nothing to change these.

It may be conflict inside yourself. Perhaps you feel you ought to do something but you don't want to. You may have mixed feelings about someone or something and not know what to do.

All you can do is try to examine yourself and do what you feel is right.

It may be helpful to talk to someone about it.

It may be that you feel hopeless in a situation. Try to be realistic; make a list of all the characteristics of the situation and of yourself and then face the facts.

Perhaps you feel weak, inferior, not good enough, ignored or guilty. Once more, try to be realistic. It may be true! If it is true it may not really be so serious. But it may not be true or it may not be as simple as you think it is. We sometimes only see our own position in a situation. It may well be that other people also have their own problems or are also guilty, etc. You may be able to change your view of the situation by re-defining it, and saying quite simply, 'Oh, it could be worse' or 'Well, there's another side to it.'

Perhaps you have several different problems. Try to see them separately and deal with them one by one.

Perhaps you feel you have too much responsibility. Share some of it. Or just don't do something. It is amazing how life can continue if we don't do something which we thought was very important.

It may be that you are acting in a way which isn't natural to you. This may be causing you stress. Is it worth it?

Perhaps you are stressed by fears you can't identify. Do your best to decide whether they are real or not.

A few tips

★ Which of these are the five most useful ideas or suggestions for you (or, in your opinion, for a stressed friend!):

a) What is the worst thing that could happen to you in the problem you have? What is the worst thing that could happen to you generally? Is the first as serious as the second?

b) Re-define your worry as a problem. Then you can do something about it instead of just worrying.

c) Do something! It is often better to make a decision (even if it isn't the best one possible) rather than do nothing.

d) Do something before things get worse!

e) Decide what can be improved and what can't. Do something about the former and accept the latter.

f) Find something else which interests you. This may make your problem less important.

g) Decide what is important to you and don't worry too much about what other people might think.

h) Talk to someone about your problem. Try to be as objective as possible, don't complain all the time!

i) When you have really done your best to solve the problem and have failed, learn to live with it. At least you know that you have done your best.

j) Make a list of all the things which are good or quite good in your life, and be pleased about those ... at least some of the time!

Old recipes for happiness

People have had problems since the beginning of time. Some proverbs are probably thousands of years old.

★ Which of these proverbs and sayings do you think are useful today? How do you interpret them?

Tomorrow is another day.

A bird in the hand is worth two in the bush.

Cultivate your garden.

Count to ten.

Walk tall.

Enjoy half a loaf.

Be thankful for small mercies.

Be yourself.

It takes all sorts to make a world.

Actions speak louder than words.

The best things in life are free.

Better late than never.

It is better to give than to receive.

A change is as good as a rest.

Don't cross the bridge until you come to it.

It's no use crying over spilt milk.

Look before you leap.

He who fights and runs away may live to fight another day.

Two heads are better than one.

Don't make a mountain out of a molehill.

Don't beat your head against a brick wall.

Don't bottle things up.

Don't always want the upper hand.

Don't wish you were someone else.

Don't underestimate yourself.

Don't refuse to listen.

Don't look for trouble.

Don't tear yourself in half.

Don't think the grass is greener on the other side.

Don't stick your head in the sand.

Don't expect life to be fair.

Don't think it's too late.

Relaxation

Mind and body

The mind and the body are not separate. When you relax your body you can relax your mind. Here are some ideas for people who find it difficult to relax. You might find it useful to do the first exercise before a difficult and stressful situation, for example, an examination or a confrontation with someone.

GOOD BREATHING

Good, controlled breathing is deep, slow and steady. If you would like to try it:

– You should try to fill the lower part of your lungs first (you can stand, sit, or lie on the floor).

– Place your hands flat and gently against the lower part of your rib cage. Your fingers should just touch.

– Breathe in slowly and naturally. When you breathe in, your abdomen should expand at the beginning of your breathing and your chest shouldn't move very much at this stage.

– Hold your breath, then let your muscles relax, and breathe out slowly and evenly. It is the breathing out which is so important for relaxation.

SLEEPING BETTER

First of all, do you really have a sleep problem? Tests have shown that people who believe they aren't sleeping enough may be getting only about 40 minutes less than the average. And, secondly, if you are sleeping badly, are you worrying about something? You must try to solve that problem before sleeping techniques will help you.

Here are some commonsense ideas. How many of them do you do already?
– If there is too much noise use earplugs.
– If there is too much light double the thickness of your curtains or wear eyeshades.
– Keep to a regular time for going to bed. The body works on a 24 hour clock and gets used to certain habits.
– If you have been sitting all day, go for a late night walk or do some exercises.
– Don't work or do anything stressful just before you go to bed. Spend some time reading a 'relaxing book', watching television, listening to music, etc.
– In bed try doing something very boring (British people imagine sheep jumping over a fence one at a time!), invent stories, recite poetry, etc.
– In bed concentrate on your body. Try lying flat in such a way that each half of your body is in an identical position. Do breathing exercises. Then concentrate on different parts of your body, starting with your toes and your fingers and trying to make each individual muscle relax.
– If you really can't sleep or if you wake up and can't sleep, it is better to accept it, put the light on and read for a while than lie there feeling very tense.

MUSCLE RELAXATION

A tense body makes a tense mind. A quarter of an hour of muscle relaxation every day will pay you well! You will gain extra energy and goodwill towards life generally.
    Try this now: tighten up your thigh muscles as much as you can and hold this tension for at least 30 seconds. Then relax and feel a delicious sense of relaxation flooding your legs!
The basic technique is as follows:
– Find a quiet room, don't have a bright light.
– Loosen your clothes, particularly around the neck and waist.

– Lie on a carpet flat on your back with your legs slightly apart.
– Tense and relax each part of your body in turn, starting with your feet and working upwards towards your head. Tense separate muscles if you can, even the separate muscles in your face.
– Finish by thinking about your whole body. Lie still for another ten minutes. Imagine beautiful places, perhaps a place in the country you know well.

MEDITATION

Simple meditation techniques are easy to do and reduce stress in many people. It is difficult for people to do if they are used to living a fast and stressful life, but it is immensely rewarding. You appreciate the wealth of your own being and are able to work even better as a result!
– Find a quiet place.
– Sit comfortably.
– Think of one thing like an object or a word. Concentrate on that one thing. If your mind wanders away, don't worry, that happens to everyone. Just bring yourself back to the object you have chosen.
– Do this for 15 to 20 minutes every day, preferably in the morning and in the evening before you eat. (Even five minutes is a help.)

SELF-HYPNOSIS

Some doctors teach the technique of self-hypnosis to their patients so that they can relax themselves if they enter a stressful period. In order to hypnotise yourself you need an open mind to the idea, and you must have time and a quiet place.
– Don't try too hard, you must feel relaxed in order for hypnosis to work.
– Sit in a relaxed position.
– Look at an object, preferably a little above you, and don't let your attention wander.
– As you look at it repeat to yourself that your eyelids are getting heavier and heavier and heavier until they close. They're getting heavier, they're getting heavier. Concentrate on the heaviness of your eyelids.
– Take a deep breath, hold it, then breathe out slowly. Say 'relax' to yourself. Tell yourself that you will relax more deeply each time you breathe out.
– Continue to breathe slowly and deeply. And continue to concentrate on any object which has a vertical sense of movement in front of you.
– You will remain in control of yourself at all times and can become your normal self by saying that you will come out of the hypnosis when you have counted from 5 to 1.
When you are in a state of hypnosis you experience deep relaxation. Furthermore, you can tell yourself what sort of things you must do in future. Speak to yourself positively rather than negatively, for example, 'I shall relax during my train journeys to work and I shall enjoy the simple things around me.'

The techniques in this section help us to value ourselves and to find belief in ourselves. They concentrate our attention on inner richness rather than material richness. Even 20 minutes each day can contribute a lot of good and reduce the stress of living in the 20th century.

How to think creatively

Left side and right side

Have you got a balanced brain?

imagination	language
music	number
rhythm	analysis
colour	reason
dimension	logic
humour	reading
	writing

Self-Portrait by Leonardo, Turin Library

Roger Sperry and Robert Ornstein of the California Institute of Technology won a Nobel prize in 1972. They discovered that the human brain has two sides, and each side has different work to do.

The left side of the brain controls language and number; it analyses and reasons. The right side controls our imagination; it controls our understanding of space and colour; it controls our appreciation of music and our sense of rhythm. It is the right side of our brain which daydreams.

Leonardo da Vinci (1452–1519), the great painter and sculptor, made use of his imagination, his sense of colour and composition and emotional feelings.

He was also an anatomist (he studied bodies by cutting up corpses and making drawings of their internal organs, muscles, bones and sinews). Furthermore, he was an architect, a scientist and an inventor!

Leonardo used both sides of his brain. And he was able to use both sides within each activity. He used his sense of size and space from the right-hand side of his brain when he was doing his

8

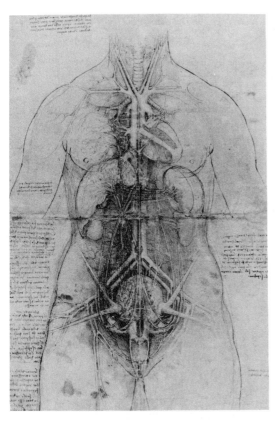

Anatomical study by Leonardo, Windsor Castle, Royal Library

Machines by Leonardo, British Museum

drawings of anatomy. But he used his sense of analysis and reason when he thought about how the body actually works. When he invented machines he used both his imaginative ability and his analytical ability.

Albert Einstein (1879–1955) also used both sides of his brain. He enjoyed art, playing the violin and sailing. Great artists and great scientists are similar, they both use the two sides of their brain. Indeed, Einstein said his scientific discoveries grew from his imagination rather than from analysis, reason and language. He said that written and spoken words were not important in his thinking. The story goes that Einstein was daydreaming one summer's day while sitting on a hill. He imagined that he was riding on sunbeams to the far distance of the universe. Then he found that he had returned to the sun. So he realised that the universe must curve.

He got this idea by using his imagination. He then used the left side of his brain to apply analysis, number and reason. And finally he used language to explain it.

If you have two legs why hop?

Traditional, established education in schools encourages us to use the left-hand side of our brains. Why don't we give more value to visual thinking? Language, number, analysis and reason are given more importance in our schools than imagination and daydreaming.

We are encouraged to hop when we have two perfectly good legs!

We all need both sides of our brain. We need to use our imaginations to think of solutions to problems and to enjoy emotional and artistic experiences. And we need to be logical and to be able to analyse and organise in order to survive day by day.

★ Here is a very easy experiment for you: next time you have a meal, first of all think of the balance of food on your plate. Is there protein (meat, beans)? Are there too many fats in the food (pastries, cakes, sweets, fried food)? Are there minerals and vitamins (fruit and vegetables)? Is it a well-balanced meal? Now think what you must do after your meal, plan your time. You have been using the left-hand side of your brain. Now use the right side of your brain! Enjoy the sight of the different colours and shapes on your plate. Look at the textures of the different foods and at the way the sauce moves. Smell the food and enjoy the many different smells. Feel the different textures and temperatures in your mouth. Now you are using the right-hand side of your brain!

It is true that some people find it easier to use one side of the brain rather than the other but we can all use both sides and we all benefit by using all the powers we possess. Nietzsche, the philosopher, said that we add to our knowledge by making conscious the unconscious.

DOES LEFT MEAN BAD?

In Latin the word 'left' is 'sinistra'. And the word 'sinister' in English means 'wicked' or 'villainous'. Does 'left' mean 'wicked'?

People with original and powerful imaginations have often been attacked in the past (and are often attacked or laughed at today!). New and fresh ways of looking at things are disturbing for us. Ideas and the 'laws' are challenged and disturbed. The left side of the brain is upset! People in school who daydream and use their imagination are often told that they are lazy. And yet their dreams can change the lives of everyone round them.

Three 'thinking' languages

We solve some problems by mathematical thinking, some problems by visual thinking and some by verbal thinking. And we solve some problems by making use of all three! Would you add a fourth or fifth type of thinking language?

Can you recognise which 'thinking' language to use at the right time? Can you use all of these languages? Which is your best 'thinking' language?

★ Here's a problem. Which 'thinking' language do you need?

Imagine a large piece of paper. It is as thick as this page. Imagine that you cut it in half. You put one half on top of the other. Now, you cut both those in half and put the four pieces one on top of the other. You continue until you have cut the paper 50 times. (Actually, this would be impossible to do! But imagine it!) How thick is your pile?

The first cut doubles the thickness of one piece of paper (2 × 1).

The second cut doubles the thickness again (2 × 2).

The third cut doubles it again (2 × 2 × 2).

And 50 cuts give the amazing figure of 1,000,000,000,000,000.
(If the paper is as thick as typing paper then it will be 80,000,000 kilometres thick – more than half the distance from the earth to the sun!)

Which 'thinking' language did you use for this problem? When I began to think about this problem I used visual thinking. I 'saw' the sheets of paper increasing in thickness. I realised that they were doubling. Then I changed to mathematical thinking and quickly realised that the thickness would be enormous! Then I changed to more technical thinking and I used my calculator. Verbal thinking wasn't very useful in this case.

★ Here's another problem. Which 'thinking' language do you need?

When Alex, Brian and Chris finished their race they were feeling tired. It had been raining very heavily, so heavily in fact that the judge was unable to see who came in first, who second and who third. When he asked the three men, they each made two statements. One man lied in both his statements. The other two told the truth. This is what they said:

Alex said: 'I came in first. Chris was last.'

Brian said: 'Alex wasn't first. Chris came in second.'

Chris said: 'I was before Alex. Brian wasn't second.'

So what was the order in which they crossed the finishing line?

This problem needs your verbal thinking language. (The answer is on page 84.)

★ Here is another problem:

The security guard at the local bank spends the evening till midnight in the manager's office. He then goes to bed in the store room. In theory he should pass through all seven doors in the bank, locking each one behind him. In fact this can't be done and he is always getting confused. The manager has therefore decided to build an eighth door so that he *can* pass through all the doors in succession, locking each one behind him. He isn't quite sure where to put it, however. Can you help? Remember the guard must start from the office and pass through every door *once* only before going to sleep in the store room.

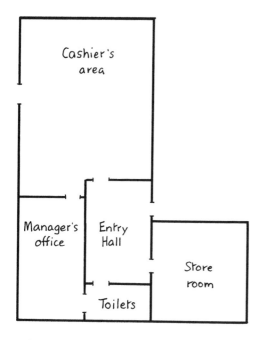

(The answer is on page 84.)

★ And a fourth problem! Now you'll need mathematical thinking:

Two young men start a new job in an office. The manager tells them they will start with £4,000 a year paid every half year and have a choice of:
– a rise of £50 a year, or
– a rise of £20 every six months.
One of the young men chooses the first option, the other the second one. How can you explain the fact that the manager gave the job that involved more responsibility to the young man who had chosen the second option? (The answer is on page 84.)

How to develop your visual thinking

Verbal and mathematical thinking are given a lot of attention at school and college. Visual thinking using the right side of the brain, is not given very

much attention or value. Indeed, according to W. Gray Walter, the famous neurologist, one sixth of normal people rarely use visual images in their thinking. (He also says that two thirds of normal people do sometimes use visual imagery and one sixth make a lot of use of visual imagery.)

It is because many people don't make full use of their powers of visual imagery that I am devoting a section to it.

Seeing objects in your mind's eye

★ Look at these designs for two minutes and then see how many of them you can remember. Draw them out even if you do it quite roughly.

★ Make a doodle. Look at it for two minutes and then see if you can draw it from memory.

★ Can you imagine an apple (or other fruit you know well)? Look at one for a minute.

What colour was the apple? Was it coloured? Where was the apple? Was it on a table, in a basket, on a tree ...?

★ Which of the objects listed below can you see clearly in your mind? Can you describe them?

The front of your house

Your bed

A telephone

The number 'two'

A friend's face

A well-known politician

I find this exercise quite difficult. What about you? Could you see pictures for each object or only for some of them? Could you see them all very clearly or only vaguely?

Obviously some people can remember and see in their minds better than others. But we all have astonishingly good visual memories. If we didn't we wouldn't be able to find our way home or recognise old friends!

Seeing actions and movement in your mind's eye

★ Try to imagine these actions:

You arrive home, you go to your door, put your key in the lock and open the door. You take off your coat. You go into the kitchen and you make yourself a drink.

Could you see these actions in your mind's eye? It is a useful technique and one which can be improved with practice.

If you lose something it is a good technique to reconstruct your actions until you remember what happened to your lost object. Recently, for example, I couldn't find the garage key. I thought back to the last time I had used the key.

I tried to see, in my mind's eye, all my actions in detail: I came home, put my bike into the garage, I locked up and put the key ... ha! into my anorak pocket!

★ Try this. Take one part of your day, yesterday lunchtime, perhaps. See if you can remember exactly what you did.

★★ Alternatively, choose an experience you share with a friend or neighbour (in class, at home, etc.). Try to reconstruct every possible visual detail of it with them.

This is also a useful technique if you can imagine a possible sequence of events in the future. For example, we see a saucepan on the stove, then a child comes into the room. Although the child isn't near the stove we stand up and move the saucepan further back from the edge. We have seen in our mind's eye what might happen.

Doctors, surgeons in hospital, engineers, cooks and drivers must all be able to see pictures in their mind's eye. A sequence of actions may be important to them but so also may the ability to predict alternative shapes or alternative three dimensional forms.

This is a Chinese tangram puzzle. The art of using the tangram is to use all the seven pieces to make a variety of different pictures or patterns. Here are two pictures, both made with the same seven pieces.

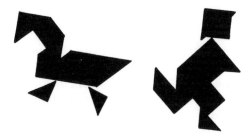

★ Can you imagine how the pieces are arranged? If you really can't imagine it then make yourself a tangram out of paper and try it by 'seeing' rather than by 'imagining'.

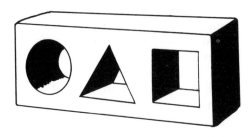

The diameter of the circle, the base of the triangle and its height, and the square sides all have the same dimensions.

★ Imagine a single, solid object that will pass through each hole. It must fill the holes and not let any light pass through. Try first of all to imagine what shape the object would have to be. Then try sketching objects to see if that is easier. Finally, make a copy of the block in cardboard and try cutting shapes until one goes through all of them. (See the answers on page 84.)

Here's another example of a three dimensional challenge to your imagination.

★ Look at each pair of dice. Which of the first dice can be turned so that they are in the same position as the second one? (See the answer on page 84.)

AFTER LEUNG

Jokes often depend on people's ability to see a picture in their mind's eye. And if the picture is ridiculous, perhaps impossible, it will make people laugh.

15

Hearing, smelling, tasting and touching ... in your mind

Can you hear things in your mind's ear? Can you smell things in your mind's nose, taste things with your mind's tongue and touch things with your mind's finger tips?
Can you hear the wind through the leaves of trees?
Can you smell your favourite food?
Can you taste a creamy ice cream ... or a bitter fruit?
Can you touch a rough, woollen jersey ... or a silk shirt?

★ Try this. Ask someone to read these sentences to you very slowly. Close your eyes and see if you can hear, feel, taste and smell in your mind. (If you can find someone else to listen and imagine at the same time you will be able to compare your experience.)

'Imagine pulling on rope. You hear the roar of the sea. Your bare feet are on the hot sand. There is the taste of salt in the air. Now, you are no longer pulling, you are waving. The hot, soft sand is changing into hard, rough concrete. The sea no longer roars, you hear screeching brakes of cars before they crash.'

Which sense could you imagine most easily: seeing, hearing, smelling, tasting or touching?

★ With a friend take it in turns to suggest sounds, smells, sights, tastes and things to touch.

We don't make enough use of our ability to imagine the whole range of our sensations. With this sort of practice it becomes much easier.

Creating new objects and actions

Creative thinkers must be able to imagine objects, people and scenes.

They must also be able to imagine alternatives and new combinations and connections. We can all do this, although many people believe they can't! It is probably because many societies don't value this ability enough. Societies often give more value to memory of facts and figures and to verbal and technical skills. The examples below include ordinary, everyday ideas and images from fantasy worlds!

★ Try this. Imagine a flag blowing to the right ... then imagine it changes and blows to the left. Imagine the flag is red ... imagine it changes to yellow ... imagine that blue starts at the bottom and slowly moves up and replaces the yellow.
Imagine a stone dropped into a pond. Ripples spread across the surface of the pond. Imagine a much bigger stone and the splash and the waves in the pond.

★ Try this. Imagine that a person or an object in the place where you are now becomes smaller and smaller ... until it is very small indeed. Now imagine the person or the object becomes bigger and, for example, is crushed up against the ceiling. Imagine part of the person or object becomes longer ... much longer. Imagine taking the small object and placing it somewhere else. Imagine the three images (the small one, the big one and the one with the long part) all in front of you and arranged together.

★ Try this. Imagine a tree growing by a road. The tree rises out of the ground. Earth and stones scatter and fall. Then the tree bounces down the road.
Did you see this picture in your

mind's eye? You have never seen it with your 'real' eyes. Visual thinking can help you to see things you have never seen.

★★ Here's another experiment. A washing machine. You open the door and the clothes fly out gracefully. They dance in the air in front of you.
Can you see this? Describe the washing to a friend.

AFTER-IMAGES

Was it difficult for you to imagine the various objects and scenes in the previous section? You may believe that you aren't capable of imagining anything! If you think this it is probably because you have lost an ability which you once had. I believe you can re-discover that ability if you want to. In the two experiments below you will see an after-image. The images are not in your imagination, they are actually in your eye. However, they will remind you of what imaginative inner pictures are like.

Experiment 1

1 Get a piece of bright green paper. Cut out the shape of an elephant. Put a black dot in the centre of the elephant, and then put the elephant on a dark background. Make sure that everything is brightly lit. (If you can't get a bright piece of green paper you could draw the elephant with a green felt tip pen. Make it a clear, flat colour even if it isn't very well drawn. Or take another bright coloured piece of paper and cut the elephant out of that.)
2 Stare at the dot on the elephant for ten seconds. Don't move your gaze.
3 Then look at a plain white wall or a piece of white paper and you will see a large pink elephant! Alternatively, you can close your eyes and see a small pink elephant!

Experiment 2

1 Look at the centre of the Shri Yantra Mandala.

2 Breathe through your nose, flaring your nostrils, six times. Breathe out through your mouth, slowly, six times.
3 Close your eyes and look upwards at the back of your forehead. The after-image which forms there is like the sun. Use your imagination and will to colour it.

HYPNOGOGIC IMAGES

Most children and many adults (70–80%) see hypnogogic images and yet they are never talked about. And most people don't even know they are called hypnogogic images!
Most people see this type of imagery just before going to sleep or when emerging from sleep. We can't control hypnogogic imagery; the images are

sometimes like the things we have been looking at during the day, for example, if we have been working in a garden we might see flowers, trees or bushes. Sometimes they are strange images which we could never have seen before.

Some people can see such images at any time, they only need to close their eyes. Some people see bright, clear naturalistic pictures and some only see patterns of colour or light and dark.

Various artists have said that they have used their hypnogogic images in their work, for example, Richard Wagner, Edgar Allan Poe and Lewis Carroll. And the contemporary novelist, Ray Bradbury, has described how he has woken up, seen images and made notes on them immediately.

William Blake, the English poet and painter (1757–1827) said that he once saw an angel sitting in a tree. He thought the angel was really there and not in his imagination. Perhaps it was a hypnogogic image? Blake often used the images that he saw in his mind as the basis of his paintings. In his picture 'The Angel of Revelation' Blake has illustrated the image (was it a hypnogogic image?) which St John saw when he wrote the Book of Revelations in the Bible. St John was living and working on the island of Patmos when he saw a giant angel in the sky, 'his face was like the sun and his legs like pillars of fire'.

The Metropolitan Museum of Art, Rogers Fund, 1914

I often look at pictures in my mind. Here is an illustration of a picture I remember.

Very often my picture changes as I look at it. At first it may include memories of the scene in front of my eyes. Then the objects change, some disappear, others grow stronger and new objects join them. When objects change they often remain a similar shape. For example, I once saw an eye which changed into a turning globe of the world which then turned into a cabbage.

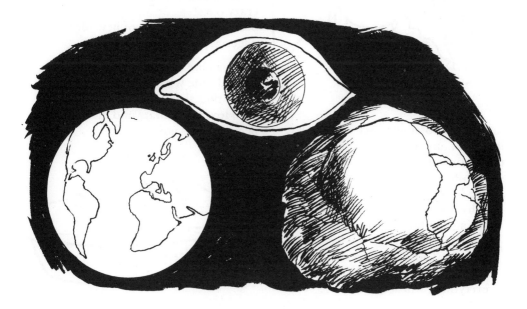

Have you ever seen hypnogogic images or do you see them regularly? Do you know anyone (else) who has seen them? What are they like? Are they naturalistic or abstract patterns?

★ Why not try looking for them before going to sleep tonight?

In bed you must relax, not only your body, but your mind. Think gently of things which aren't verbal, for example, the countryside, or a slow, relaxing hobby. Your verbal mind makes it difficult for your non-verbal mind to become creative. If you usually fall asleep very quickly then here's a trick! Lie with one arm bent upwards from the elbow. If you fall asleep your arm will drop and wake you up! Have a note pad and pen by your bed and be ready to describe any images you see so that you can read them or show them to a friend in the morning.

In fact it is possible to see hypnogogic images at any time. If you are in a quiet place now you might be able to see something if you close your eyes and have a look.

★ Why not try it? Make sure you are sitting comfortably and that no one is going to interrupt you for a few minutes. Close your eyes and even cover them with your hands. At first everything will seem dark ...

without anything there at all! But you may see small pin pricks of light or some variations in the darkness. Look at them and ask yourself if they look like anything you can recognise.

For many years I have encouraged people to try to re-discover this ability to see images which they certainly had as a child. At first most people say they can't do it, but all they need is encouragement and practice to find again this wonderful power which we all have.

Techniques for creative problem solving

P I E

When you have a problem think of PIE!

P = problem
First of all, define the problem (see opposite).

I = ideas
Then imagine a lot of ideas – even crazy ones!
See How to get a lot of new ideas on page 22.

E = evaluate
Now decide what value the ideas have – and then decide!
See How to evaluate and make a decision on page 31.

Define the problem

★ What is it? Can you see the duck or the rabbit? It is very difficult to see both. Once your mind is fixed on one idea it is very difficult to start again.

Nowadays we know that the moon is a sphere, we can see that it is. But for centuries most people didn't *see* the sphere because they *thought* it was flat.

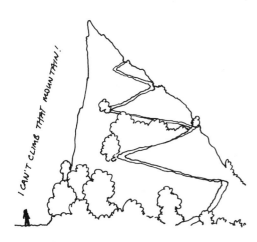

STAND BACK FROM THE PROBLEM

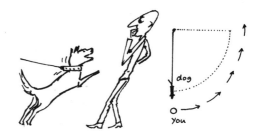

Stand back from the problem and you will see more useful information.
★ Try this puzzle. Draw four straight lines (only four and don't lift your pencil from the paper) which will connect all the dots:

```
o    o    o

o    o    o

o    o    o
```

Do you find it difficult? If you find it difficult it is because you aren't standing back from the problem! (The answer is on page 85.)

WHAT REALLY IS THE PROBLEM?

Often it is more important to examine the problem than it is to look for an answer. Sometimes you find there is no problem at all!
Problem: The television doesn't work. I can't mend it.
Examine the problem: I don't necessarily need to watch television. Really I only need some entertainment. So I can play a game with my children or read a book or go and see my friends. Suddenly, there is no problem!
   Try to define what you really want. But are you sure you are defining your true objectives?

Problem: You want to give your friend a copy of a new record which has just been released. You go to the shop but they haven't got it. Do you feel angry or disappointed? Do you leave the shop? Or do you look around? They have another record which you are sure he or she will like. It might be even better!

You know that your real objective is to give pleasure and surprise rather than one particular record.

Here are two typical problems. I have tried to re-define them so that they don't seem so bad! Try to re-define the third one yourself.

Problem 1: I haven't got enough money.

Re-definition: I want to buy more things than I really need.

Problem 2: My boss doesn't seem to appreciate me.

Re-definition: I don't appreciate how many problems my boss has.

★ Problem 3: The next door neighbour plays his music very loud. How can I stop him? How can I stop hearing his music?

★★ Write down two or three problems. Try to re-define them. Or you might write down two or three of your own problems and ask a friend to re-define them. You can then discuss with him or her if their re-definition is helpful.

How to get a lot of new ideas

OTHER PEOPLE'S GOOD IDEAS

At school we learn about other people's good ideas. We study the great poets and the great scientists and we are expected to know what they did and what they said. We have to learn enormous quantities of this information for examinations. We are rarely encouraged to have our own ideas and, in any case, there is no time for them. Our ability to experience life freshly, our ability to find alternative ways of dealing with challenges and problems is usually very limited because of this.

The creative person is always ready to change his or her ideas and to challenge the ideas of other people and society. The creative person feels that life is unique and rich with new possibilities. And I believe we all have the ability to experience life in this way.

But how do we rediscover this potential in ourselves after so many years of education and examinations? Even in a few minutes it is possible for people to see something of their potential. Of course, it takes time to develop this potential so that it can become a way of life.

THE FAMILIAR STRANGE OR THE STRANGE FAMILIAR?

When we are in a strange situation we look for things we recognise and understand. We try to make the strange familiar. This is a sensible and useful thing to do. However, it can prevent us from seeing the potential of a new and strange situation.

Correspondingly it should be possible for us to see situations we know well in a new way, to see the familiar as strange. Most problems aren't really new. But can we look at them in a new way?

Here are some experiments. They should help you to experience the familiar in a new and fresh way.

Experiment 1

Sit down (if you aren't already seated!)

and relax. Make up sentences which describe what you are aware of and what you feel at this moment. For example, I can hear a car passing in the street. I am aware of the heaviness of my body on the chair and of my arms on the table. I am aware of the stillness of the room and the activity of my mind.

It's interesting to know what you are aware of. We rarely stop to give attention to ourselves and to our surroundings.

Looking, thinking and contemplating are important for all creative people. Picasso said, 'For me creation first starts by contemplation, and I need long and idle hours of meditation. It is then that I work most. I look at flies, at flowers, at leaves and trees around me. I let my mind drift at ease, just like a boat in the current. Sooner or later, it is caught by something. It becomes precise. It takes shape . . . my next painting motif is decided.'

Experiment 2

Once more, make sure that you are relaxed and free to 'lose' yourself in thought. Look at an object. You might, first of all, look at its shape, both at its general shape and at the shape of each of its parts. Let yourself be distracted by the colour, or by marks on the object, or by patterns. Let your eye gaze at the object and let your mind contemplate it . . . and don't feel the need to hurry.

William James said, 'If we wish to keep our attention upon one and the same object, we must seek constantly to find out something new about it.' For many kinds of problem solving it is essential for us to be aware of the character of the objects in the situation.

Experiment 3

Children don't need to look between their legs to see the world in a new way! Adults do! If nobody is looking at you at the moment then why not stand up and look at the world upside down?! (Careful not to become dizzy!) Do things seem different? Do the colours seem richer and the shadows deeper? Do some familiar shapes seem strange? Alternatively, use a hand mirror to study your room.

Experiment 4

Use your imagination to see the ceiling as the floor and the floor as the ceiling.

Experiment 5

Words are very important in our thinking, but sometimes they are given too much importance. They dominate other ways of thinking. For example, we always want to name objects and categorise them according to names. In the room where you are now it would be very easy to categorise all the furniture together. Try to categorise the objects around you differently, try to categorise them according to their qualities, for example, their colour, their pattern, what they are made from, whether they are vertical or horizontal, rough or smooth.

BRAINSTORMING

We all feel like this sometimes. But what about inventors, designers and problem solvers? What do they do when they are trying to get some new ideas?

Designers often use the well-known technique of brainstorming. It is very good for getting a lot of ideas in a short time, and is enjoyable to do.

What you need

You should have about six or seven people. (It is more dynamic and good fun with a group of people. Less than four and more than 15 may be difficult.) The people should know each other and they should feel comfortable. There should be a relaxed, even a happy atmosphere, and everyone should sit in a circle. Then make sure that everyone knows what the problem is.

What you do

1 Tell the group that they should:
– think of as many ideas as possible; the ideas should be connected to the agreed problem but can be silly or sensible
– never criticise other people's ideas at all (or even think of criticism)
– listen to other people's ideas and suggest ideas which might be connected
– feel quite free to say the most ridiculous ideas
– produce as many ideas as possible

2 Start with a 'fun' problem. This will make everyone relaxed and inventive. For example:
Ideas for selling beds.
How to help someone who can't sleep. There has been a mistake and one million eggs have been delivered to a local shop; what should they do with them?

3 The brainstorming should last about 15 minutes. People can either shout out their ideas or write them down and then pin the paper to the wall for other people to see.

4 Then people look through the ideas and discuss them. Always look for the possible uses of an idea, even if it seems quite silly.

★★ Here is a brainstorming activity for you to try with your friends. Plan an unusual holiday which both you and your friends might enjoy.
Don't forget: worry about practical matters afterwards!

SLEEP ON IT!

Other people find that stopping work and going for a walk round the garden or talking about something different has the same effect and a solution to the problem suddenly comes to them.

ANALOGIES

An analogy is the relationship between two things which are similar in one or several ways. There are many well-known analogies. For example, the analogy of a tree with the relationship between various languages:

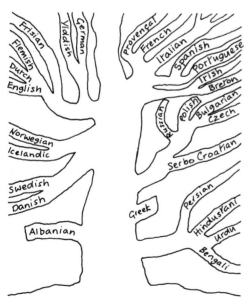

We can think about a tree and understand the relationship between the roots, trunk, branches and twigs and this helps us to understand the relationship between ancient and more modern languages.

Here are some well-known analogies. Do they exist in your language?

1 When you are planning.
Analogy: Building a house. (Make sure the ground is firm and suitable. Make sure you build solid foundations.)
2 When you intend spreading an idea.
Analogy: Farming. (Make sure you prepare the ground and sow the seeds at the right time.)
3 When you intend to persuade people.
Analogy: Warfare. (Plan your campaign. Get your weapons ready. Retreat. Trap the other person. Hammer the point.)

Well-known analogies (and clichés, metaphors, stereotypes, sayings and proverbs) may actually make it difficult to look at information in a new way. For example, the analogy between warfare and persuasion: the problem solver may think that peaceful ideas are impossible! Can you see any disadvantages in analogies 1 and 2 above?

I hope this section will help you to look for new, original analogies which will give a new and original view of the information and the problem you are dealing with.

Sheila Blakeney is an Industrial Designer who needs to think of new ideas to solve problems as part of her job. She says:

'When I can't think of an idea I go into one of the big stores in town. I wander about looking at anything at all. Then I often, suddenly, get an idea. I will see a connection between an object I am looking at and the problem I am working on. And this connection might give me a new idea. For example, a seaside town has asked me to design them some new litter bins. The problem is that the seagulls can reach inside the bins and remove the litter. I know that if I put a lid on the bin people will be lazy and not bother to open it.

I couldn't solve the problem so I went into town. As I went into a big store the door opened automatically as I came to it. I had walked through a light beam and this light controlled the door. Now I am working on a design in which the litter bins will open as people go past. I'm making the bins amusing, for example, big frogs, so that people will even look for litter so that they can have the fun of throwing it inside!'

Here is another example, a problem of a social kind. David S. describes his problem:

'I work in an office, in a firm which sells furniture. I hate the work I do, because I don't need to use any intelligence or have any ideas, and I'm not learning anything. Also, the other people treat me as if I have no brains at all!'

This analogy might help David with his problem:
A filing system is an analogy for people's minds. People have a filing system in their heads.

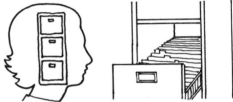

And all the information they see, hear, feel, touch and smell is put into their filing system. If they can't find the file for the information they throw it away (forget it). And when they have put some information in a file they don't want to move it, as they haven't got the energy to move it. Advice to David S: 'People in your office have put you into their filing system. And the file with you in it is marked "Office Boy".'

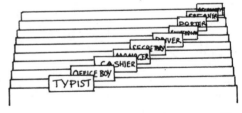

They expect you to behave like an office boy. They don't think you can type, they don't think you can manage!

If you want to improve your job you must make them put you into another file or change your file.

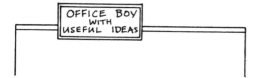

Buy journals about the furniture industry and read them at home. Read about new inventions, new materials, new fashions. Then talk to the other people in the office about them. Ask questions, even make suggestions. You might see a news report in the local newspaper about a new hotel or a new housing estate. Suggest that the firm tries to sell their furniture to these people. Keep jumping out of your file with good ideas and they will have to re-file you.

★ Here is another problem. Read about it and then see if you can use the suggested analogy to find an idea for a solution. If you want to find an alternative analogy, then do!

Problem: A college tutor is worrying a student. The tutor asks questions, not to help the student but to prove to him how foolish he is. The tutor enjoys playing with the student and isn't concerned with the subject at all.

Analogy: Cat and mouse. (For a way of using this analogy see my suggested answer on page 85.)

UNEXPECTED CONNECTIONS

Open a dictionary at any page, take any word and see if you can connect the word to the problem. You might see the problem in a new way. For example:

My neighbour's son is 18 years old, he is going to college in October. Although my neighbour is proud of his son he feels very critical of him because he doesn't study and, indeed, he doesn't do much work at all for the family. Most days he stays in bed until midday!

This is a problem! We talked about the problem for some time but we couldn't look at the problem in a new way. I suggested that we use dictionaries to help us! My neighbour picked up the *Collins English Dictionary*, closed his eyes, and let it fall open. He waved his finger around and then let it fall on one of the pages. His finger fell on 'help'.

help (hɛlp) *vb.* **1.** to assist or aid (someone to do something), esp. by sharing the work, cost, or burden of something: *he helped his friend to escape; she helped him climb out of the boat.* **2.** to alleviate the burden of (someone else) by giving assistance. **3.** (*tr.*) to assist (a person) to go in a specified direction: *help the old lady up from the chair.* **4.** to promote or contribute to: *to help the relief operations.* **5.** to cause improvement in (a situation, person, etc.): *crying won't help.* **6.** (*tr.*; preceded by *can, could,* etc.; *usually used with a negative*) **a.** to avoid or refrain from: *we can't help wondering who he is.* **b.** (usually foll. by *it*) to prevent or be responsible for: *I can't help it if it rains.* **7.** to alleviate (an illness, etc.). **8.** (*tr.*) to serve (a customer): *can I help you, madam?* **9.** (*tr.*; foll. by *to*) **a.** to serve (someone with food, etc.) (usually in the phrase **help oneself**): *may I help you to some more vegetables? help yourself to peas.* **b.** to provide (oneself with) without permission: *he's been helping himself to money out of the petty cash.* **10. cannot help but.** to be unable to do anything else except: *I cannot help but laugh.* **11. help a person on** *or* **off with.** to assist a person in the putting on or removal of (clothes). **12. so help me. a.** on my honour. **b.** no matter what: *so help me, I'll get revenge.* ~*n.* **13.** the act of helping, or being helped, or a person or thing that helps: *she's a great help.* **14.** a helping. **15. a.** a person hired for a job; employee, esp. a farm worker or domestic servant. **b.** (*functioning as sing.*) several employees collectively. **16.** a means of remedy: *there's no help for it.* ~*interj.* **17.** used to ask for assistance. [Old English *helpan;* related to Old Norse *hjalpa,* Gothic *hilpan,* Old High German *helfan*] —'help·a·ble *adj.* —'help·er *n.*

My neighbour immediately said, 'Help. It's quite right, I need help from him in the house!' I suggested, 'Perhaps your son needs help in order for him to help you? Perhaps he needs time and needs you to discuss things with him?' My neighbour then took the *Longman Dictionary of English Idioms*, closed his eyes, and let the dictionary fall open. His finger fell between 'a pain in the neck' and 'at pains'.

PAIN

on/under pain of Ⓟ at the risk of suffering (a punishment, difficulty, etc.) if something is not done exactly as ordered, promised, etc.: *Each man is strictly confined, on pain of expulsion from the union, to one type of operation....* (Eckersley, Kaufmann, and Elliott) ‖ *they were made to promise under pain of death never to enter the country again* [Adv 1, 2, 3]

a pain° in the neck *coll* 1 a person or thing that is very annoying: *Anna is a dainty blue-eyed eight-year-old with an IQ* [INTELLIGENCE QUOTIENT] *of 168. 'She's a pain in the neck, a horrible child,' says her mother...'She must know everything, win every argument and every game.'* (*Daily Mirror* 19 Nov 74) [N 3] Also (*impol sl*): **a pain in the arse** 2 **give°** Ⓘ **a pain in the neck** to annoy (someone) very much: *I feel guilty about being bored by Holmes and not liking Marlowe or laughing at Wooster. But Jeeves gives me a pain in the neck....* (*The Guardian* 15 Mar 75) [V] Also (*impol sl*): **give°** Ⓘ **a pain in the arse**

PAINS

at pains making an effort or working hard (to do something): *she seemed at pains to impress him with her knowledge* ‖ *He was at no great pains to narrate his travels or to communicate his impressions of distant lands to Mrs Penniman....* (Henry James) [Adj 1: foll. by Infin]

take° pains to be very careful (over a job, duty, etc.); make a special effort (to do something correctly): *he took pains to explain to me that I was not being dismissed because my work was bad but because the company could not pay my wages* [V: usu. foll. by Infin or over/with + Ⓟ] **~painstaking** showing or needing great care or attention to detail [Adj 1, 2]

I asked him what he thought of these idioms. 'Well, there is a danger that I think of my son as "a pain in the neck". But what he needs is to learn to be "at pains" to make an effort. And perhaps I should be "at pains" to help him to understand this!'

I have tried the technique of using dictionaries quite often. At first it seems rather silly. However, the definition of the idea in the dictionary makes me think. I try to search for a connection. And when I search for the connection my own commonsense and understanding come forward.

In ancient Greece people often went to Delphi for advice. The advice they received was usually unclear, but it could be understood in various ways. It therefore became the responsibility of the person to think about the advice and to relate it to the problem and to make the decision. At the entrance to the temple two words were cut into the stone, 'Know yourself'. The Greeks believed that individuals must be responsible for their own actions.

There are a number of famous stories about the advice given in Delphi. King Croesus went to Delphi for advice. He was told that if he crossed the River Halys, the frontier with Cyrus the Great's territory, he would destroy a mighty empire. He decided to cross the Halys and he did destroy a mighty empire. Unfortunately, it was his own! The advice seemed to be clear but it still required Croesus to think about it and he didn't.

This is what the technique of using the dictionary does . . . it makes you think, perhaps in a fresh way.

★ Try the technique yourself. You are certain to have a problem!

ATTRIBUTES

An attribute is a characteristic of a person or a thing. Robin Haywood who teaches Industrial Design students says:

'When the students can't think of anything new we sometimes use the "Attributes

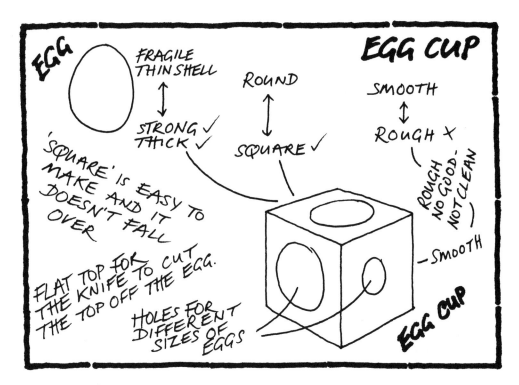

Technique." If you start with an existing object you list all its attributes. For example, at the beginning of a new academic year in September the studio is empty and not very friendly. The students don't like working in it. So last year, we tried the "Attributes Technique".

The students listed about 20 attributes of the studio, for example, flat, white, hard walls. They then wrote down several alternatives to each attribute. For the walls they wrote: angled, curved, rough, dark, coloured, bouncing, noisy.

We then went through all those characteristics and chose a few of the alternatives. In the case of the walls, we chose: angled, curved, dark, coloured and bouncing! The students then made out of wood, plastics and paper new angled and curved surfaces, and they used rubber and old car springs to make some of the areas bounce and move about! The students found that the studio became a more friendly and interesting place to work in as a result of this.'

So this is the technique:

1 List all the attributes of the object, for example:

physical – colour, weight, size, smell, surface, movement
psychological – fear, friendship
social – attitudes to it, fashion, value
economic – cost

2 Then write next to each attribute several alternatives.

3 Choose one or a few of the alternatives and you will have a new object!

The 'Attributes Technique' can be used by everyone, not only industrial designers and it need not be used for objects. For example, it could be used when choosing a dress, choosing furniture, wallpaper, or curtains for a room, planning a garden, planning a special meal, or planning a party.

★ Try this. Take one of the examples above and try the 'Attributes

Technique' on it. See if you can invent something quite new!

★ Now try this exercise. Write down everything you can about a brick: its appearance, weight, strength and surface. Does it hold water or resist water? Does it hold heat or lose it? What about the economic value of a brick? What about the normal uses of a brick? What about the beauty of a brick? What other connections can you make with a brick?

★ And now try the same exercise against the clock. Write down every possible idea for using a brick. Give yourself five minutes exactly!

If you have more than 20 ideas – GREAT!

If you have between 10 and 20 ideas – WELL DONE!

If you have between 5 and 10 ideas – OK!

If you have between 1 and 5 ideas – BETTER LUCK NEXT TIME!

If you have no ideas at all – GOSH!

Sometimes we may not want to start with an object alone but with material as well. So the 'Attributes Technique' must be slightly different. For example, if students are trying to design a new chair in wood and steel they should list all the attributes of wood and steel. They must include the idea of a tree, roots, leaves, growing, photosynthesis, seeds, etc. They must also include all the social connections with wood, for example, 'He is as thick as two planks' i.e. not very intelligent. 'She is as graceful as a willow tree.' 'He is as strong as an oak.'

They might list woods, forests, . . . and fairy tales; giants and goblins. They should list everything they connect with wood and then do the same for steel. (You might like to try

this for steel.) As they think of these attributes they should think of how they might apply them to a chair. For example, one student may like the idea of designing 'goblin chairs' for children! The technique can lead to really fresh ideas!

MORE TECHNIQUES

Modify

Change one part of the object, technique or idea. Change the colour, the shape, the sound . . . Design a car in the shape of a sphere. Could you use some of the qualities of the sphere in your car? There might be advantages but would there be any disadvantages?

Exaggerate

Make it thinner, lighter, faster, quieter, simpler, more complicated. Make it much smaller, take parts away from it.

Substitute

Imagine someone else doing the job. What would happen? Imagine a different material being used. Substitute a totally different method for doing something, normally used for different purposes.

Rearrange

Change the order of events. Change the parts of the object and make a new arrangement.

Reverse

Imagine the opposite. Imagine it to be light if it is heavy, loud if it is quiet, expensive if it is cheap. Imagine it upside down, inside out, back to front. Think of the opposite of your problem.

Then think of ways of answering that problem. It might produce some useful ideas.

Combine

Combine aims and try to answer them together. Join different methods for doing something which would normally never be used together. Put different objects together and see if they suggest a completely new object.

Too much action

Think of ideas which would make the problem worse.

No action

Think of reasons for doing nothing about the problem at all.

VAGUE IDEAS ARE USEFUL

Fixed, neat and tidy ideas prevent our minds from wandering and thinking of other possibilities. Clear ideas can actually prevent the birth of new ideas. In art and design courses the lecturers usually avoid a clear instruction! They either put questions to the students or give them general help or even contradictory advice. The students suffer! But they become used to living in the world of vagueness, multiple meanings and possibilities. It is the normal world for creative people.

When several designers are working together one may offer an idea. He or she may say, 'We've got to start somewhere. Here's an idea to kick around.' It's a sketch, which might suggest all kinds of other ideas. It can be changed until the finished idea looks quite unlike the first sketch.

★ Try this. Give yourself five minutes. List as many particular problems as

you can. (Don't generalise, for example, don't write down 'pollution' or 'wars'.) Here are a few to start you off:
– socks which always seem to be inside out
– being woken by an alarm clock
– early sunshine waking me up
– dogs which attack me when I am jogging

Use the techniques above and see if you can find some solutions.

How to evaluate and make a decision

You have examined your problem and all the information connected with it. You have thought of a variety of solutions and, indeed, you feel quite pleased with yourself because you have thought of so many ideas! But the time has come to make a decision!

Things to think about before you make a decision

1 Limitations: of time, money, technical equipment, qualified people, natural resources, goodwill of the people concerned . . .
2 How much time have you got to make the decision? Is it essential for you to make the decision now? If you can wait then the problem itself might even go away or, at least, change. If you don't need to rush the decision then you have more time to get it right. You might even be able to try out an

idea and see if it works before you really commit yourself.

3 Who will be affected by the decision? Will you have enough time to ask them what they think about it? What will happen if you don't ask them? Who is going to carry out the necessary action? Are they prepared, able and willing?

4 What difficulties will there be: from other people, institutions, society, rivals?

5 How long will your idea take? Will the results come in a few hours, days . . . or will it be years before you know whether it is successful or not?

6 What will happen if it fails? Have you got an alternative plan?

SOME WAYS OF MAKING DECISIONS

Throwing the dice

Major commercial, political and personal decisions are sometimes made by someone throwing a die, tossing a coin, or choosing a straw to see who gets the shortest one. There are circumstances when this is a very reasonable way of making a decision. If there is a choice of equally pleasant or equally unpleasant alternatives then why spend time and energy searching for minor advantages and disadvantages?

★ Try this. Write down six things that you would find very nice if they happened to you. Then throw a die and see which one chance has chosen for you. You would like it, but you might spoil it by thinking of

all the other things which you haven't got!

The least trouble

You may not like using any of the more thoughtful methods described, and you may not like working very hard to carry out a solution, so you will choose the solution which causes you the least trouble.

★ Which of the choices in the list below would cause you the least trouble?

You think you are catching a cold.

1 You do nothing about it.

2 You wear warm clothes.

3 You don't go out and you keep your room warm.

4 You go to the doctor and get some medicine.

When you have chosen one of them write down every reason you can think of to justify your decision. When you argue for one particular solution you may begin to see whether it is a good idea or not.

Act it out

In this method you list the alternatives and then you list all the good points about each one.

★★ Find a friend who will listen to you. Take each alternative and pretend that you believe in it. Argue for the good points.

Afterwards you may know which alternative you felt happiest to argue for. There may not be an obvious right or wrong decision to be made. Most decisions depend on the individual and his or her feelings and circumstances.

★ What would you do in this situation?

Your uncle dies and leaves you some money (as much as you earn in a year).

1 You put it in the bank.
2 You start a small business.
3 You take a good holiday and promise yourself several more in future years.
4 You buy an expensive object.
5 You give it away.

Instead of arguing for the good points you might choose to argue for the bad points for each alternative. The advantage of arguing for the bad points is that you will know that the alternatives you aren't taking aren't very good, and you won't feel so bad about not being able to do them!

Concentrate on one benefit

You decide to make one point very important. For example, you are shopping and you decide to buy the cheapest of everything, or you decide to buy only those things which will last a long time. This is a useful method for deciding what to do quickly, and it assures you of getting a basic benefit.

★ What single benefit would you choose for the following:
1 If you were buying a bed.
2 If you were planning a holiday.
3 If you had to choose someone to go on holiday with.

Basically OK

You take the first solution you find which contains your basic requirements. There may be others which are more attractive but you don't really care. This method gives you a quick decision without too much effort.

★ Would you want to apply this method to any problem? Which of the problems below could you apply it to? And what would your basic requirement(s) be?
1 Choosing a marriage partner.
2 Choosing a place to live.
3 Choosing a breakfast cereal.
4 Choosing a book to take on holiday with you.
5 Choosing a job to apply for.

One version of this method is to concentrate on avoiding disaster! As long as you avoid disaster you don't care what happens.

As near to perfection as you can get

List all the benefits you think you would get from a perfect solution. Ignore realities as you make this list. Then choose a solution which offers the nearest to your dreams!

This is a method which is often used. Some people choose a marriage partner in this way. And yet it is very dangerous. Having thought of your ideal you may never be satisfied with the compromise you finish up with! If you think you can forget the ideal once you have decided what to do then it is a reasonable method.

Here is an example. An 18 year old student has just passed her advanced level examinations at school. She has passed in Geography, History and French. However, she didn't do very well in French and this means that she can't go to university to study French. She could go to college and study to become a teacher (and this would mean that she could study French part of the time) or she could get a place at a university, studying Geography with small units of study in History and French.

★ Imagine she asked you for advice. You decide to use this method. What questions would you want to ask her?

Being a pessimist

When you have your list of alternative solutions you imagine all the things that could go wrong. This is a powerful method as it makes you think of real life and not of your dreams. On the other hand, if it becomes more than a method and becomes your general approach then you will never do anything. You will always see too many disadvantages.

Here is an example. Imagine that you are offered a one year travelling scholarship. All your travelling expenses will be paid wherever you go. Unfortunately, it means giving up your job (although your employer thinks you can probably get it back again). It also means that you will not see the person you are hoping to marry. These are some of your choices:

1 Accept the offer and go. Just write to your beloved.

2 Accept the offer and go but make sure that the study you do helps you get your job back. Just write to your beloved.

3 Marry quickly and go with her/him.

4 Marry quickly and leave her/him behind.

★ Can you list any more alternatives?

What are all the things that could go wrong in each case?

Giving points

The British consumer magazine *Which?* examines products which are for sale. It describes their qualities and gives points for the standard achieved. These qualities and standards are then listed in a table. Here is a version of such a table done by an ordinary shopper who is trying to make up his mind what sort of home computer to buy.

	Computer 1	Computer 2	Computer 3
keyboard		✓	✓
reliability	✓	✓	✓
available software	✓	✓	✓
price	✓		
memory	✓	✓	
quality of the graphics	✓		✓
repair services	✓		✓
available extras	✓	✓	✓
appearance	✓		
	8	5	6

According to this table the shopper should buy computer 1. However, he doesn't want to! Why? Because he says it is most important that the keyboard is a standard design and that it is reliable and that there is plenty of software available for it. So, in fact he should have made a table with points.

For example, he might have listed the qualities in order of importance and given them points:

keyboard . . . 3
reliability . . . 3
available software . . . 3
price . . . 2
memory . . . 2
quality of the graphics . . . 2
repair service . . . 1
available extras . . . 1
appearance . . . 0

This would then give a different result! For example, the reliability of computer 1 is not known so, of the maximum of three points, only one has been given. The price of computer 2 is high so it does not get either of the two points available to it.

	Computer 1	Computer 2	Computer 3
keyboard	0	3	3
reliability	1	3	1
available software	2	3	1
price	2	0	0
memory	2	2	0
quality of the graphics	1	0	1
repair services	1	0	1
available extras	1	1	1
appearance	0	0	0
	10	12	8

This method appears to be objective. However, it only provides a rough guide. Above all it helps the user to decide on what he or she really wants.

★ Can you think of more ways of making decisions? Do you have any opinions on the advantages and disadvantages of each method?

When you try to find many possible solutions to a problem you use the right-hand side of your brain a lot of the time. (You use your imagination, you feel rather than think, you are willing to suggest ideas without worrying about their practicality, you prefer to think of complete ideas rather than of small, logical steps.) When you are evaluating the possible solutions and making a decision you make more use of the left-hand side of your brain. (You make use of logic and reasoning; you analyse, you examine parts as well as the whole, you use language and number rather than pictures, sounds and your senses generally.) The ability to be both creative and analytical lies within us all. We just need to learn to change hats!

A checklist for problem solving

My students at Manchester Polytechnic sometimes despair. They say they can't solve problems and they aren't creative!

There are many ways in which we try to help them. One way is to give them the list of questions and comments below and ask them to choose the ones they think are relevant to them. We then discuss the ones they have chosen:

obviously not all the comments are suitable for each student.

★★ Look through the list and decide if any of the questions and comments apply to you. Discuss the comments with your friends.

Do you spend enough time trying to define the problem?
Comment: Spend a lot of time thinking about the problem itself before you start thinking about the answer. A problem well understood is a problem half answered.

Do you sometimes worry about a small part of a problem instead of the main gist of the problem?
Comment: It might make you feel better for a short time. But really it is probably a waste of time... and the main problem might even become worse!

Do you think it is a good idea to collect a lot of information before trying to find a solution?
Comment: Of course, it is usually essential to collect information. But useful work only occurs when you look for relationships between the bits of information.

Do you prefer to get your information from books rather than from talking to people and from direct experience?
Comment: Books are an obvious source of information. However, sometimes you can only 'understand' information if you experience it.

Do you accept what experienced people tell you?
Comment: It is sensible to listen to the experiences of other people. However, sometimes you must reject this experience in order to have a new look at the problem.

Are you reluctant to ask people to help you?
Comment: Many people can help. Of course, experts are useful but sometimes other people can help just as well.

When you get an idea do you refuse to change your mind?
Comment: Keep your mind open to alternative ideas. Only decide when you really must do something.

Are your ideas too ambitious? (Can you achieve the idea in the time?)
Comment: Ask yourself how much time, money, etc. you have; and which idea you can do within those limits.

Do you have a fixed procedure which prevents you from discovering new, more useful methods?
Comment: Efficient, established procedures are essential. However, they often make it difficult to adapt to the individual nature of some problems.

Do you try to fit new experience into ideas that you know already and can even give a name to?
Comment: Certainly this will help you to know what to do and to make decisions. However, it might prevent you from recognising a new experience, and a new problem with very different needs.

Do you think that normal, common and obvious ideas and behaviour are usually right?
Comment: People used to think it

was impossible to fly. They used to think it normal to kill people in ceremonies.

Do you like to behave like the people around you?
Comment: It is natural to wish to belong to the group of people you like or feel safe with. However, if your problem is important you may have to do something the others don't like.

Do you think it is wrong for women to be reasonable, logical and practical? Do you think it is wrong for men to be filled with feelings, to be emotional, to show pleasure and sadness?
Comment: These values are given by society. (Certainly this is the case in the West, and society and the individual are the poorer for them.)

Are you afraid of being foolish?
Comment: New ideas are often laughed at.

Do you get depressed when things go badly?
Comment: Everybody does. But some people stop trying and others don't.

Are you afraid of failing?
Comment: When children are very young we don't mind their mistakes. Later parents and teachers don't want children to make mistakes. They often seem to care more about their children avoiding mistakes than about achievement. Many of us feel our personality is threatened if we make a mistake, and yet mistakes are an inevitable part of learning. Furthermore, we can learn by our mistakes: in that sense, mistakes are positively useful!

Do you think that ideas must either be right or wrong?
Comment: Departure times of trains must be right or we miss them!

However, for most ideas the answers may not be 'right' so much as 'the most effective we can see at the moment'.

Do you think that logic is very important?
Comment: Sometimes an answer to a problem may seem very logical. However, the basis of the answer may be at fault. Certainly logic has a major part to contribute in problem solving. However, the creative person must be able to forget logic sometimes! Logic can spoil the fun of crazy thinking which may be the only way of seeing a problem freshly.

Do you always look for what is wrong in ideas?
Comment: Of course you want to avoid dangerous or silly ideas. However, if you concentrate on what is wrong you may not see what is useful in an idea and what can be done with it. It is difficult to have two attitudes at one time. A positive attitude moves you forward and may lead to new ideas. A negative attitude stops creativity.

Do you enjoy the act of problem solving?
Comment: Solving the problem is important. But for some people the act of trying to solve the problem is exciting in itself. And it is such people who are particularly able to remain open to new and unexpected ideas.

Are you brave?
Comment: Can you reject everything you have believed in and worked for? If you can, you are a brave person, and it is good for you. Everybody makes mistakes, but some people are so unwilling to change that they prefer to live with their mistakes for their whole lives.

How to use your memory

A most remarkable memory

Shereshevskii, a Russian journalist, had one of the most remarkable memories in the world. He could remember very long numbers, long poems in unknown languages, and complicated scientific formulae for years. For example, this formula is only part of a much longer formula he remembered for 15 years:

$$N \cdot \sqrt{d^2} \cdot x \frac{85}{vx} \sqrt{\frac{276^2 \cdot 86 x \cdot n^2 b}{n^2 v \cdot \pi 264}}$$

In order to remember the formula he invented a story. Before you read the story, look at the formula and try to invent a story about it yourself!
★ How long do you think you could remember the formula?
Shereshevskii's story went like this:

Neimann (N) came out and poked with his stick (.). He looked at a dried up tree which reminded him of a root ($\sqrt{}$) and he thought, 'It is no wonder that this tree withered and that its roots were lain bare, seeing that it was already standing when I built these houses, these two here (d^2)', and again he poked with his stick (.). He said, 'The houses are old, a cross (x) should be placed on them.' This gives a great return on his original capital, he invested 85,000 roubles in building them. The roof finishes off the building (−), and down below a man is standing and playing a harmonica (vx) . . .

So, although Shereshevskii had a good memory, he also used a technique in order to improve it. It meant he didn't forget the complicated things he had learnt. The next section describes more memory techniques which might be useful to you.

You, too, have an amazing memory!

Think about how old you are, how many places you have been to, how many people you have seen in your life, how many things you have done. A lot of these events are still in your memory – somewhere deep in your brain.

Consider . . . Sometimes people survive a very serious accident or a moment of great danger. They are very near death, but they live. Very often these people say that they see all their life pass before them.

'I was on my bicycle, and I turned a corner into a main road. I must have been half asleep because I didn't notice this huge bus which was racing towards me. I knew instantly that it would hit me. There was nothing I could do. Then the whole of my life seemed to pass before my eyes.

I don't know how much I saw or how much I felt, but I seemed to experience everything. I saw myself as a little girl getting dressed; I saw myself at school, at the seaside. I saw myself as a student and meeting my husband . . . everything. And yet I only had a second to remember all these things before the bus hit me!'

Consider . . . Hypnotists can make you relax, and you can look into your memory under hypnosis. Your memories may be happy or sad or just ordinary, but, most importantly, you can remember an amazing amount of information.

Consider . . . Sometimes the smell of a flower reminds us of a holiday, sometimes a laugh, an accent, or a way of walking reminds us of a person. I am sure you have experienced something like this. It shows that your brain has remembered an enormous amount of information and one small detail brings the memory to the surface.

★ What memories do these things remind you of?
The sound of a motorcycle.
The smell of cooking.
The coldness of wind.
A bitter taste.
Do any of them remind you of a particular incident?

Do older people have good memories?

It is true that your mental abilities are at their best between the ages of 18 and 25. However, you only lose 5–10% of your mental abilities over your lifetime. So you remain a very rich person indeed!

So why do elderly people find it difficult to remember things? First of all, do they find it difficult? Is it not that they are often interested in different things to young people? They have a vast past which young people don't possess, and they enjoy looking at this past. Also, older people have found a way of living – they have established a way of life, their friends, work, etc. They don't need to learn and remember as much as younger people. However, older people who remain active in business, politics, art, or in their hobbies can learn and remember new information as well as younger people. In Britain there have been many people over the age of 65 who have begun a degree course with the Open University and passed successfully.

Active involvement, a continuous striving to understand, to organise in the mind and to make new things and produce new ideas will keep us lively, even if we have lost a few brain cells!

On the other hand, if we do what we have always done, think what we have always thought, and learn new information or skills without thinking about them, we will be old before we are 40!

Memory and remembering

Short term and long term memory

There are two kinds of memory, short term memory and long term memory. Short term memory lasts up to five or ten minutes. For example, if somebody gives you directions in the street you may remember them for a few minutes but have no memory of them later the same day.

How can we encourage information to go from our short term memory to our long term memory? How can we find the information again in our long term memory?

The mind is like a library. Some libraries are chaotic and some are well organised. In the next section there are suggestions for how to move

information from your short to your long term memory and how to find it again.

Organising your information

LOOK FOR THE IMPORTANT INFORMATION

If the information is important you are more likely to notice it and to remember it than if it is unimportant. But what is important?

★ Try this. You will need a pencil and paper. Read through the words below, but don't try very hard to remember the words.

book	river	cat
net	house	wood
man	car	bus
joke	orange	typewriter
sky	road	tea
flower	lamp	potato
table	page	spoon
arm	cloud	
Cambridge University		

Cover up the box. Now write down as many words as you can remember. It doesn't matter what order you write them in. Finished?

Compare your list of words with the words above. You probably remembered Cambridge University! It is important within the list above. First of all, there are two words and they are both long. Secondly, Cambridge University is the only proper noun in the list. You may have remembered other words because they were important to you. Can you say why they might be important?

Did you remember 'book' and 'net'? They are important simply because they are at the beginning of the list. Did you remember words from the end of the list? In short term memory we often remember the last part of the information.

★ Try this. Try to remember these words . . . then write them down.

man map cat cap tap rap lap

How many words did you remember?

Now try to remember these words . . . then write them down.

book car tree apple big hot pen

You probably remembered more words from the second list than from the first list. That is because it is easier to remember words which have a different sound.

Of course, the two activities above are only games, and you might say that it is easier to remember important things than unimportant things! Of course, what is important for you may not be important for someone else.

★★ Do you remember what your friends remember? Even if you do things together you will remember different things. If you have shared something with your neighbour (a previous English lesson, a coffee time, a film) ask what he or she remembers most from the experience.

GROUP YOUR INFORMATION

If you want to remember a lot of information try to organise it – put it into different groups, for example.

★ Try to remember the two lists of words below. Read through each list two or three times and then see how many you can remember from each list. It would be a better test if you wrote them down!

List 1

margarine mushrooms oranges bread salt milk coffee cheese pears soap meat bananas soup potatoes sugar eggs rice fish

List 2

Transport
Road: bicycle motorcycle car taxi bus coach
Rail: train underground
Air: plane helicopter balloon
Sea: ship boat yacht canoe

You probably remembered more from List 2 than from List 1. That is because the information in List 2 was organised.

You will remember the information even better when you do the organisation yourself!

★ Organise List 1 into groups, and then try to remember the words again.

★ Look at these words for a few minutes and try to remember them; then write them down.

bicycle house flower car plane garden tree bathroom guitar football bus bush chess sitting room grass tennis racket

How many have you remembered? The 16 words belong to four groups. The groups are: transport, living place, plants, hobbies and sports.

★ Write down each group and then try to remember the words again.

Make a new group

Even if the information is well organised it is useful to make a new organisation of your own. The activity of organising is a powerful help to your memory.

★ Read through the groups of words below for three minutes and try to memorise them. Then close the book and write down as many as you can.

car	carrot	chair	elephant
bicycle	potato	bed	cow
bus	cabbage	table	dog
train	tomato	desk	cat
plane	lettuce	stool	mouse

Now think of a new way of grouping these words. Write down the words in your new groups. Cover them immediately, and try to remember them. Write down the words you remember.

Useful groups

There are many ways of grouping words. The act of looking for a way of grouping the words will help you to remember them. However, the sort of grouping you choose ought to be a useful one to you. For example, food can be grouped according to:
– the shops where you will buy it
– the meals you are preparing for
– the content (protein, fats, sugars, etc.)
– the weight and how you are going to transport it and store it
– the order in which you wish to prepare and cook it

★ How many different ways can you think of grouping cars? What would be the main use for each of your groupings?

FIRST LETTERS FIRST

The first letter of a word is more important than the last letter.

★ Try this experiment. Can you think of:

A fruit beginning with the letter A?
A country beginning with the letter A?
A city beginning with the letter P?
An animal beginning with the letter C?
    Now, can you think of:
A fruit ending with the letter . . . r?
A country ending with the letter . . . n?
A city ending with the letter . . . s?
An animal ending with the letter . . . g?

    Did you find that difficult? That is because we often order information in alphabetical order, which gives importance to the first letter(s). For this reason it is often helpful to order your information alphabetically in your memory as well as in your card file.

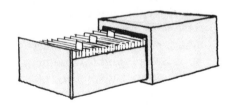

The best way to learn is to teach!

If you want to tell someone about a subject you must:
a) Study the subject.
b) Think about the subject so that you can explain it.
c) Organise it so that you can explain it.
d) Try to explain it.

e) Find out how successful you have been. Find out where you failed to explain it well.

A teacher has to do all of this, and the more successfully he or she does it the better the students learn. But in doing this, the teacher understands and remembers it very well.

You may not be a teacher. However, if you want to remember something it is a good idea to pretend you are going to have to teach it, and to go through the stages above. Make your own organisation of information, and you will increase your understanding and your memory.

Making notes

Part of a tape recording of a head teacher talking about her work is reproduced below.

★ Try to remember the various things she said so you could use them in discussion. Make five headings for the information she gives. This will help you to remember the information. (See suggested headings on page 85.)

'. . . it's not a rough school at all. In fact we never have any trouble really. A lot of the parents are very interested . . . I have to be so careful you know . . . a lot of the families are West Indian and their customs aren't the same as mine. I have told children to look at me when I am talking . . . and I noticed that West Indian children often didn't look at me and I said, "Look at me when I'm talking to you!" And they just looked down. Then I was told that that is how a West Indian shows respect . . . they don't look at you! I've got some problems with some of the teachers. Some of them believe in teaching reading, writing and arithmetic and nothing else . . . the children are aged three to eight . . . there are so many other things to learn as well . . . social skills . . . finding out about how things work for themselves . . . The school is OK I suppose . . . well, actually the building is pretty difficult and we don't have enough equipment . . . well we don't have any really! Anyway they are lovely kids! That's what matters. But I'm glad I don't have to actually teach any more. I really enjoy planning . . . perhaps I shall want to get back and teach again one day though . . .'

Making notes from books or from lectures will help your memory. When

you make notes you must re-organise the ideas, change them to a new form and make them look special and memorable. All this activity on your part will help to make the information memorable and you will have the notes to look at when you do the necessary repetition of your study. Three ways of making notes are described below.

FULL TEXTS

Full texts copied from books or essays you have written are not as helpful as structured notes. The information isn't divided into groups which can be remembered. Here is part of a full text copied out by a student:

Publishing Books

Why do you want to publish a book? That is the first question to ask yourself. Writing and publishing books is a long and demanding business. A book may take you several years to write and several years to publish. So, it's a good idea to know just why you want (or if you want!) to spend so much time and energy trying to do it! Do you want to make money, to be famous, to change the world a little, to express yourself, to enjoy making an object? And are these strong enough reasons to keep you going for a year or two?

Who is the book for? Is your book for a special interest group or just people generally? Is it for 8-9 year old children who have a learning difficulty or is it for people generally who might like to know about a particular hobby?

What about a publisher? Why should a publisher want to publish your book anyway? Will they make money from your book? Is there a big enough market? Are there any other books on the same

subject? Would the book be the right sort of
book for the publisher?
(There is no point in sending poems to a publisher
of novels.)

STRUCTURED NOTES

Here are the points which have been
made in the text above:

Publishing Books
Motive for writing
· Writing and publishing takes
several years.
· A strong motive is needed
e.g. creativity, money ...
Buyers and readers

· General or special
interest?
Publisher's interest

· Money or prestige
· Existing series
· Big enough market
· Few competitors

It is easier to remember the points
when they are listed like this.
Furthermore, you have to find a new
and fresh way of expressing the points
when you want to communicate them
to someone else. There are various
techniques which can be used to divide
the notes into groups:
– titles, sub-titles
– the use of CAPITAL LETTERS
– the use of Capital and Small Letters
– the use of underlining
– the use of colour for the words or for
underlining

– the use of different strengths of line
for your writing

important/not impt.

– the use of different strengths of line
for underlining

_____

_____

| | the use of dividing lines and occasionally of boxes around information |

_____

– note that the use of some thick and
some thin lines is not only useful but
attractive
– the use of a narrow column for the
main notes. The space on the left of
this column can then be used for extra
observations, for later remarks, for
references, for numbering, etc. This
white space also offers a space for your
mind to relax in! There is nothing
worse than a tightly packed page of
text which offers no hope of a rest!

NOTE MAPS

A different way of arranging your notes
may be more suitable for some
purposes and/or for some people. This
technique of 'note mapping' helps you
to group your information, to relate the

groups of information in various ways
and helps you to make a memorable
'picture' of the notes.

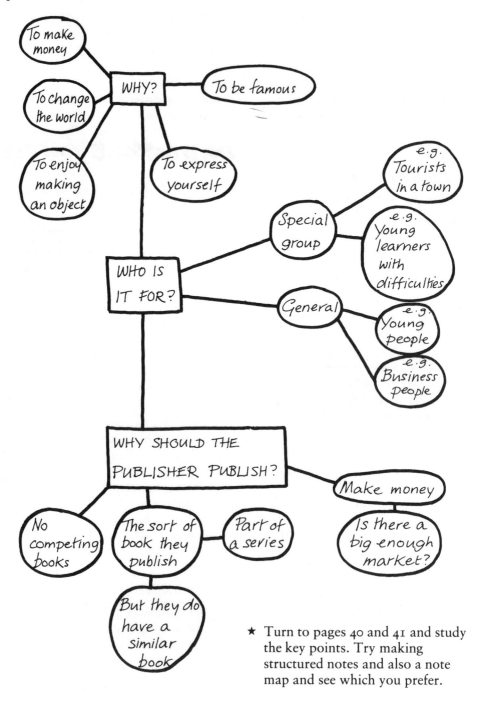

★ Turn to pages 40 and 41 and study
the key points. Try making
structured notes and also a note
map and see which you prefer.

Organising yourself

HAVE A BREAK!

Do you study all day without stopping?

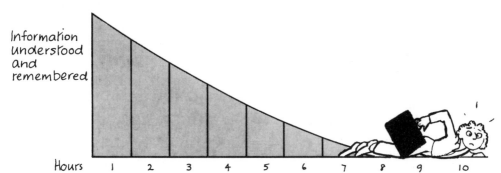

Can you really sit and study your books all day without stopping? Do you want to say you have worked hard? Or do you want to understand and remember?

Do you study for two or three hours . . . and then stop?

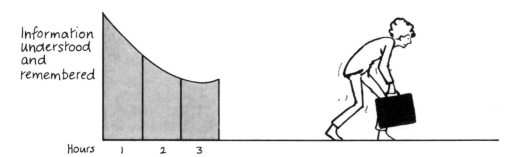

Why not work all day with breaks?

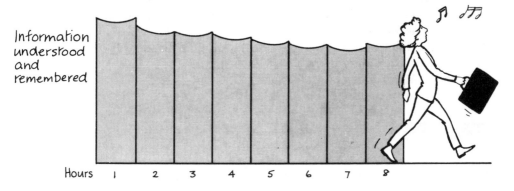

Your attention is high at the beginning and just before you stop. So, why not have a break quite often – about every half hour? Then you will continually keep your attention high.

However, during your break don't do any other difficult work, or you will forget everything!

★★ Try this game which demonstrates how easy it is to forget information in your short term memory if you try to think of something else. You will need someone to help you.

Say any six letters, slowly, to your friend and tell him or her to remember them. For example, M . . . S . . . B . . ., etc. (Make sure they don't spell a word!) Now, immediately ask your friend to count backwards, in threes, from 100 as fast as possible. Hurry your friend up all the time! 100, 97, 94, 91, 88, . . . After 30 seconds ask your friend to tell you the six letters! He or she has probably forgotten them. The letters were in short term memory. They weren't fixed in his or her long term memory and you have pushed them out!

Of course, this is a simple little game. However, the principle is the same for more serious information.

A LITTLE AND OFTEN IS BEST

The Post Office wanted to teach postmen to type, and asked Mr Alan Baddeley (Director of the British Medical Research Council's Applied Psychology Unit in Cambridge) to advise them. Alan Baddeley decided to organise the postmen into four groups:

| I hour per day | 2 x 2 hours per day | I x 2 hours per day | 2 x I hour per day |

In 55 hours the first group had learned as much as the second group in 88 hours! And they were continuing to learn faster. Furthermore, several months later, the first group had remembered more than the second group. So, the principle is: work for a short time every day rather than a long time occasionally.

KEEP GOING BACK

This is what happens if you don't go back:

After a short time you know more and can remember more because you have sorted out the information. But by the end of the day you have forgotten most of it!

Go back and study your notes or your books or video after a short interval of 10 minutes to two hours,
THEN AGAIN after one day,
THEN AGAIN after one week,
THEN AGAIN after one month . . .
three months, nine months.
This is what happens if you do go back:

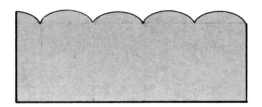

After a short interval look back actively at your notes, rearrange them, re-write them, re-structure them. Spend about ten minutes for each hour you have worked.

After one day see how much you can remember without looking at your notes. Then go back to your notes with the particular purpose of looking for what you have forgotten. You can rearrange your notes again. You will find it useful to explain what you have been studying to another person. Your friend will make you do your best!

If you revise after one week, one month, three months and nine months you will remember the information!

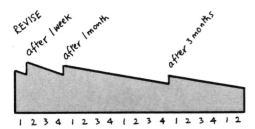

You don't need to spend very long – a quick test, a quick glance through your notes.

Important Note 1
It is important to remember each major point of information. Otherwise you can't connect the new information to anything.

Important Note 2
Your brain is bigger than your stomach! You can never fill up your brain like a stomach or a filing system. A well organised memory increases the memory. Experience shows that it is easier to learn new foreign languages when you know several already.

Learning new vocabulary

Technique 1

This is an example of the 'keep going back' technique:
1 Learn a word / Teacher: Rabbit is le lapin
2 Test it / Teacher: What is rabbit? / Student: Le lapin
3 Learn a second word / Teacher: Cat is le chat
4 Test it / Teacher: What is cat? / Student: Le chat
5 Test the first word / Teacher: What is rabbit? / Student: Le lapin
6 Learn a third word / Teacher: Dog is le chien
7 Test it / Teacher: What is dog? / Student: Le chien
8 Test the first word / Teacher: What is rabbit? / Student: Le lapin
9 Test the second word / Teacher: What is cat? / Student: Le chat
10 Learn a fourth word / Teacher: Mouse is le souris
11 Test it / Teacher: What is mouse? / Student: Le souris
12 Test the first word / Teacher: What is rabbit? / Student: Le lapin
13 Test the second word / Teacher: What is cat? / Student: Le chat
14 Test the third word / Teacher: What is dog? / Student: Le chien
15 Test the fourth word / Teacher: What is mouse? / Student: Le souris
Why not try this method with your

own new vocabulary in English? The technique is that you:

1 Repeat the new words frequently.
2 Increase the time between each repeat and test.

Technique 2

If you are learning a list of new words, try this:

1 Read through the words slowly, twice.
2 Test yourself.
3 Read through the words again.
4 Test yourself.
Etc.
The technique is to repeatedly: learn, test, learn, test, etc.

Both these techniques are mechanical. You don't have to think about the meaning of the words nor use them to express your ideas. If you learn the words like a parrot then you will use them like a parrot!

The mechanical techniques described above may be helpful for some people. But no one can really learn the meanings of words until the meanings are thought about!

We learn words in our own language by hearing them or reading them. If we are interested in the information they communicate we want to know what the word means. As we meet the word more frequently in different situations we get to know it just as we would get to know a person, by meeting them. And, of course, we use the word. If the effect is right on the other person then we know we are using it correctly. If it is a useful word we keep on using it and finding out its different meanings. This is the ideal way for us to learn the words in a foreign language. However, there is often not enough time to learn

ARE YOU LEARNING LIKE A PARROT?

in this way. We are expected to learn '20 words for homework'! So, are there ways in which we can make this learning of 'words for homework' a little more like learning our own language?

In the previous section it was suggested that 'grouping' and 're-grouping' words according to various meanings will help us to remember them. Here are some more ideas on how to make words meaningful to us so that we can learn them and learn how to use them.

STARTING POINT

I am going to assume that you have been asked to learn 10 to 20 new words in a foreign language. You have a list of them and the meanings in your own language. I am also going to assume that you can learn the words like a parrot in order to use them like a parrot, if you wish. However, you must think about the words if you are going to use them thoughtfully! Listed below are a number of ways in which you might think about the meaning of the words and make yourself work with them. It is the difficulty of doing the work which will help you to remember them. The principles are: grouping and re-grouping, personal associations, strange connections.

★★ If you use some of these activities with a friend or neighbour you will remember the words better because you have to think about their meaning and communicate with and about them.

FAMILIES OF WORDS

There are various ways of grouping words. And the same words can be grouped differently. Can you re-group the words in the example below? Compare your grouping with your friend's grouping.

book
magazine
newspaper
letter
advertisement
cartoon
photograph

film
video

painting
sculpture
drawing

Grammatical categories

You might group according to grammatical category (nouns, adjectives, etc.).

he
she
someone
them
us

think
throw
sleep
love

slowly
thoroughly
deeply

a an the

red
old
angry

Families of meaning

Animals
dog
cat
cow
horse
sheep

Plants
tree
grass
flower
vegetable

Companions

Some words are often used together, for example, drive/car, wave/goodbye. (These are called collocations.) You may find some words in your list of words which go together. Or you can combine a word you know already which collocates with the new word.

You could list the collocations and then ask your friend which of the new words you are thinking about. Here are some examples to try: traffic, fruit, bread, flower, motorcycle, car, football match, shop, holiday, book.

Associations

Some words remind you of other words. Other people may not have the same associations. In the diagram below I have joined together the words which I associate together. For example, I associate 'cat' and 'cow' because of life on a farm. But I also associate 'cat' and 'boat' because sailors used to take a cat with them to catch the rats. See if your friend can guess the associations which you make with these words.

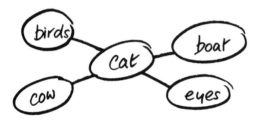

Feelings and associations

Which are your favourite words and which don't you like? You can express your feelings about what the word looks like or about what it means. Compare your feelings with your friends. Do you agree with my choice?

like
duckling
crocodile
fish
hedgehog
smile
umbrella

don't like
block of flats
vet

Synonyms

You may find that some of the words you must learn mean the same thing. Or you may already know another word which means the same as a new word you must learn. Write the new word with a synonym and learn them together. (Note that some words can mean different things. You may only know one or two of these alternative meanings. When you choose a synonym it may only share one of these meanings. For example, 'part' can mean the same as 'depart', or 'divide' or 'piece', but 'depart', 'divide' and 'piece' do not mean the same thing.) Do you know synonyms for: big, happy, sad, ship, reply, request, go back, right, road, save, entertain? Work out the synonyms and then ask your neighbour to say which words he or she thinks you started with.

Similar words

Some words are not quite synonymous. It is a good idea to put these words together because they make you think about the differences. And if you have to think you are likely to remember. For example, 'talk', 'speak', 'say', 'express'; 'shoe', 'slipper'. It is a good idea to try to find a sentence for each word and to think about the differences.

Antonyms

'Like' and 'dislike' are antonyms (as are 'tall'/'short', 'sweet'/'sour', 'happy'/'sad'). Note that 'tall'/'short' and 'short'/'long' are antonyms, but 'tall' and 'long' are not antonyms. What are the antonyms for: open, strong, rich, fast, noisy, certain, often? See if your neighbour can guess the words you began with.

Parts of words

Can you divide the words into different parts? You may be able to find a prefix or a suffix in the word, for example, 'un' is the prefix of 'unhappy'; 'ness' is the suffix of 'softness'. If you can learn what these prefixes and suffixes mean you can use this knowledge in understanding, remembering and using other words.

Definitions

It may help you to think of a definition of the new word. You could make this definition in your own language. Ask your friend to say which word you have tried to define. Which words do these definitions define? 'To hit something with the foot.' 'To plunge head first into water.' 'To exchange something for money.' (See answers on page 85.)

Examples of use

It may help to think of a sentence (or several sentences) in which the meaning of the new word is very clear. Can you find an appropriate sentence or sentences for 'send'?

A memorable story

Try to use all the words you are trying to learn in a memorable story. The story should be ridiculous and impossible so that you will remember it! Exchange stories with your friend.

It was very hot. I wanted some refreshments. I knelt down to drink and saw my reflection in the water. Then I saw my hair! It was awful. The hair-dresser had ruined it. I wanted my revenge.

I decided to ruin his reputation. I wrote to the local newspaper and recommended the hairdresser to everyone: I said he was remarkable! I enclosed a photograph. I thought everyone would be shocked and refuse to go to his shop. Unfortunately, it has become the latest fashion and everyone is respectful to him ....

... and to me !!

A development

You might be able to connect all or some of the words as part of a 'development', for example:

school
|
book
|
paper
|
tree
|
country
|
earth

Can you arrange the following words into a 'development'? Doctor, farmer, man, woman, boy, girl, hen, egg.

Connections

You connect one word to another like stepping stones. You have to know what each connection is. You could do this as a game with your neighbour.

Here are some words for you to connect: actor, tomato, pub, bed, run, match, café, work.

Rhyming words

Can you think of words which rhyme with the new words? Can you even write a poem?

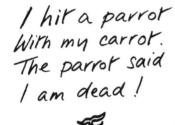

I hit a parrot
With my carrot.
The parrot said
I am dead!

Can you think of words which rhyme with: hat, she, nose, dog, speak, year?

Mime

Can you mime so that a friend can guess which word you are thinking about? Try: hole, lid, parcel, punish, remain, take.

Pictures

Can you draw a picture which illustrates the new word? It is easy enough to illustrate 'horse', but can you illustrate 'love', 'stop', 'unhappy', 'justice', 'guilty'? It doesn't matter if no one else can recognise your drawings.

WHICH PICTURE ILLUSTRATES FEAR AND WHICH ILLUSTRATES PRIDE?

Cognates and false friends

A cognate is when a word in a foreign language means the same as the word in your own language. In German 'Haus' and 'Mann' mean the same as in English. But 'bekommen' in German doesn't mean 'to become', but 'to get' or 'to receive', so it is a false friend.

However, it is possible to use a 'false friend' in order to remember the meaning of a word. For example, the word 'Schrank' in German means cupboard or wardrobe. An English-speaking person might remember the meaning of 'Schrank' with the sentence, 'My jeans shrank so my mother put them in the Schrank!'

Memory techniques

THE ADVICE OF ST THOMAS AQUINAS

St Thomas Aquinas, the famous Christian philosopher (1225–74), thought that a good memory is part of good sense. He gave the following advice:

There are four things which help a man to remember well.

First: Arrange things in an order.

Second: Think about the information and ideas with all your attention.

Third: Connect them to unusual things.

Fourth: Repeat them frequently.

How to remember a list of objects

TECHNIQUE 1: STRANGE CONNECTIONS

Recently, my neighbour amazed me by his memory! He asked me to list 15 words. He then told me to try to remember them and he would do the same. I could only remember four – but he remembered all 15 – and in order!

★ Try it yourself. Look at these 15 words. Try to remember as many of them as you can. Give yourself two minutes.

boot	flower	knife
watch	page	cook
hand	school	television
car	water	glasses
chair	apple	bird

How many did you remember?

1–5 words   fair
6–10 words   good
11–12 words   very good
14–15 words   excellent

Here is how my neighbour did it. (Now I know the technique I can remember 15 words as well!) It is an old technique, described below, and when you have learned it you will be able to:

– remember 15 words
– remember them easily
– remember to remember them in order
– remember them in any order!

But first you have to do a little work! It might seem difficult but thousands of people have managed it. And think about how you are going to amaze your friends! The technique is adapted to the individual person, so now I want to help you to make your own technique.

The numbers 1–15 follow. Look carefully at the shape of each number and try to imagine an object which looks like the number. Then write down the name of the object. (You might have to use your dictionary to find the English word!) If you can't think of an object which looks like the number then choose an object which you connect with the number. Here are various examples. In some cases I couldn't find an object which looked like the number, and I have marked these with a *. You only need one object for each number. These are just examples.

1 pencil	2 swan	3 ace of clubs
4 boat	5 star	6 elephant's trunk
7 flag and flag pole	8 two eggs	9 pipe

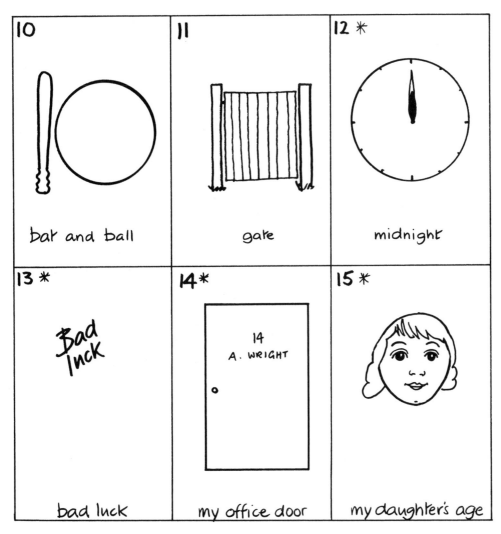

10	11	12 *
bat and ball	gate	midnight
13 *	14*	15 *
bad luck	my office door	my daughter's age

Decide which picture *you* want to remember for each number. Now test yourself. Close this book and write down the numbers 1–15 and see if you can imagine the picture you have chosen for each number. When you think you know them . . . test yourself with the numbers in any order. For example, what are your objects for: 3, 14, 7, 12, 6, 15, 2, 9, 4, 1, 8, 5, 10, 11, 13?

Now you know your objects very well. You will remember them for years and years! You are ready! Here is how to apply the technique:

★★ Your friend has asked you to remember 15 words. Here they are:

1 cup	9 cat
2 hammer	10 bottle of milk
3 head	11 football
4 carpet	12 tent
5 flower	13 fish
6 pilot	14 bicycle
7 bell	15 post office
8 egg	

Here is the technique. You must imagine your friend's object and your object together. Imagine a ridiculous connection or an amusing connection. It is always difficult to remember ordinary objects and events. Some people say it is easier to remember an action in the picture.

Now he tests you:

You should be able to remember each combination of objects quite easily. Here is my combination of objects for the above list of words:

1 cup	2 hammer	3 head
4 carpet	5 flower	6 pilot
7 bell	8 egg	9 cat
10 bottle of milk	11 football	12 tent
13 fish BAD LUCK!	14 bicycle	15 post office

When you demonstrate this technique to your friends:

1 Ask your friends for 15 names of objects.

2 Tell them to write down the names.

3 As they tell them to you, say that they should try to remember them.

4 When they have given all the names tell them to write down all the ones that they can remember. It will be very few!

5 Then you must give them all 15 in order.

6 Then tell your friends to ask you to give the words in any order!

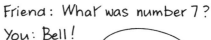

Friend: What was number 7?

You: Bell!

AMAZING!

Alternatively, instead of remembering a number of pictures of objects you might find it easier to remember this 'poem':

One is a bun

Two is a shoe

Three is a tree

Four is a door

Five is a hive

Six is sticks

Seven is heaven

Eight is a gate

Nine is a line

Ten is a hen

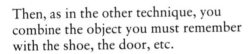

Then, as in the other technique, you combine the object you must remember with the shoe, the door, etc.

TECHNIQUE 2: THINK OF A ROOM YOU KNOW WELL

Think of a room you know very well. Imagine you come through the door. Is there some furniture on your left? Is there a chair, a chest of drawers, a cupboard, perhaps a picture on the wall? Move around the room in your imagination. See each piece of furniture.

Now, you must remember this list of words: lamp, shoe, lion, paper, girl, TV, boat, cat, fork, book, tube of toothpaste, watch, chimney, hand.

Here is the technique. Imagine the

lamp connected, in some way, with the first piece of furniture. The connection should be absurd, perhaps impossible, then you will remember it.

Super technique 2

If you want to remember 50 objects, then imagine ten pieces of furniture in your room. Don't choose furniture with a simple shape, for example a waste paper basket. You must be able to connect five objects with each piece of furniture. So, this is what the chair would look like:

Your chair seen from one side . . . and from the other. I have taken the first five objects and put them, in order, around the chair: 1 lamp, 2 shoe, 3 lion, 4 paper, 5 girl. I have made the girl very small so that I will be able to remember her better. (I might be able to remember her better if she were to move, perhaps to dance.) You then continue like this, connecting five objects with each of the ten pieces of furniture – and you will be able to remember the 50 objects.

Storytellers in the Middle Ages (12th to 15th centuries) used to remember their church. They would connect each part of their story with a part of the church. This technique is not only helpful for lists of objects but also for sequences of actions, events and procedures.

How to remember abstract words

Words which name objects are easier to remember than words which name ideas (love, history, knowledge, etc.).

★ How many words can you remember from each list? Read through the first list for one minute. Then test yourself. Do the same with the second list.

List A: book   hat   cup   elephant   radio   chair
List B: love   history   peace   cost   distance   idea

How did you do? Most people remember more words from the first list; abstract words are more difficult to remember.

In the past, teachers and storytellers remembered abstract words by imagining a symbol for each idea. Below are some ancient and modern symbols for ideas.

How many traditional and contemporary pictures or symbols can you think of for abstract ideas?

How to remember long numbers

If you want to remember a long number you should space it out and divide it into 3s or 2s, for example: 798 864 905 36. Can you remember it?

★ Try this number! But don't divide it into 3s! 83219765421

What is the longest number you can remember?

1528
67218
95061
813298
3704624
26396701
752143642
56097439485

★ Try to remember the numbers without dividing them into 3s or 2s and then try to remember them by dividing them up!
★ Write out ten numbers with 11 or 12 digits. Try to remember five of them by grouping the digits into 3s, and five by grouping them into 2s. See which is the more successful grouping for you!

How to remember people's names

Oh, I just can't remember names!

Your name is very important to you. In some ways it is you! It isn't pleasant if people forget your name; you may even be annoyed. Can you remember other people's names? Have you ever been in the embarrassing position of introducing two people who you know quite well, and suddenly your mind goes blank, and there is a short moment of panic before the names come to you? Or have you ever introduced them by the wrong name?

Before I describe some techniques for remembering faces and names, here is some advice:

1 Listen! When somebody says their name you must listen to them. It is difficult to listen because you are looking at them.

2 Say the person's name as soon as possible. For example, repeat their name the moment you are introduced, 'Oh, hello, David, I'm very pleased to meet you.'

3 If you can't spell their name ask them to spell it for you. Write it down. They will be pleased.

4 If it is an unusual name or if you connect it with another country or with an interesting connection, ask them about it. For example, people might say to me, 'Andrew, that's a Scottish name, isn't it?'

5 Most importantly, continually make use of their name. Most people like that, and it helps you to remember it. For example, if I have to remember the name of the person 'Mick' I might repeat it like this:

John: Andrew, this is Mick. Mick, this is Andrew.
Andrew: Hi, Mick! Nice to meet you.
Mick: Hi!
Andrew: Do you live near here, Mick? etc.

To use the techniques there are two essential steps you must take:

– You must notice something about the person which is easy to remember; this might be the person's face, body and movement, voice or character.

– You must then connect the name with this very characteristic which you have noticed.

Here are some examples of the techniques.

BODY AND LETTER SHAPE

Several children live in my street, and one of these is a girl aged about ten. She is thin and has long red-brown hair. She is called Hannah. I can remember her name because the letter H looks like her – long, thin legs and long, thin arms:

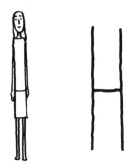

FACE

Study the person's face. Choose a characteristic part of it. Exaggerate that part in your imagination. Then connect that to the person's name. For example, I know a woman with a rather long nose, she's called Barbara . . .

I can imagine a longer nose . . .

I know the famous story books about Babar the Elephant . . .

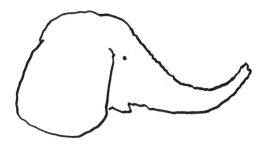

So, I look at Barbara, I see her long nose and I imagine it longer. That reminds me of Babar the Elephant. And I say, 'Oh, hello, Barbara!'

VOICE

Some people have a good memory for sounds, and they notice the different sounds of voices. Sometimes you can find a close connection between the sound of someone's voice and their name. For example, I know someone called Marigold Jones. She has a deep, rich voice, and I think her name sounds deep and rich too. (A marigold is a simple yellow-golden flower.)

CHARACTER

One of my colleagues is called Robin. He is friendly and always hard working. He has a strong sense of pride towards his work and, if necessary, he will fight for what he believes in! He reminds me of how robins are friendly to gardeners but are ready to defend their territory.

NAME

Perhaps the person has the same name or shares at least one name with a well-known person. This amazing coincidence will obviously help your memory.

Agatha Christie, Margaret Thatcher, Orson Welles, Bob Hope . . .

Perhaps the person has a name made up of English words which you know.

Armstrong, Bacon, Bell, Cage, Campbell, Day, Dark . . .

Perhaps the person has a name with a nice sound. Rhythm, sound contrast and alliteration are easy to remember.

Arnold Wesker, Jilly Cooper (rhythm)
James Thurber (sound contrast)
Alison Armley, Peter Parker, Ralph
   Richardson, Siegfried Sassoon
   (alliteration)

Poems

Ancient stories were told, learned and re-told for hundreds of years. In most cultures the storytellers were respected and regarded as very important. Before the time of books storytellers were the only way in which societies could remember their past and their stories and beliefs. The great storytellers could tell stories for hours, day after day; they could remember thousands of lines.

Most ancient stories were in poetic form. The poetry made them beautiful and easier to remember.

The Knight's Tale

PART 1

Stories of old have made it known
   to us
That there was once a Duke called
   Theseus,
Ruler of Athens, Lord and Governor,
And in his time so great a conqueror
There was none mightier beneath
   the sun.
And many a rich country he had won,
What with his wisdom and his troops
   of horse.
He had subdued the Amazons
   by force
And all their realm, once known
   as Scythia,
But then called Femeny. Hippolyta,
Their queen, he took to wife, and,
   says the story,
He brought her home in solemn
   pomp and glory,
Also her younger sister, Emily.

We still use poetry in order to remember vital information. Here are some well-known memory poems; they aren't as beautiful as Chaucer's *Canterbury Tales* or Homer's *Iliad*!

I before E except after C!

Every English child learns this at school. It helps them to remember this strange example of English spelling: a piece of cake NOT a peice of cake, ceiling NOT cieling!

Thirty days have September,
April, June and November.
All the rest have thirty-one,
Excepting February,
Which has twenty-eight alone.

Red sky at night
Is the shepherd's delight.
Red sky in the morning
Is the shepherd's warning.

If the sky is red at night the weather will be dry the next day. If the sky is red in the morning the weather will become worse.

In 1492
Columbus crossed the ocean blue.

Note the reversal of the position of the adjective blue in order to make a rhyme!

Divorced, beheaded, died,
Divorced, beheaded, survived!

The fate of the six wives of Henry VIII of England.

Warm, wet, westerly winds in winter.

Winter conditions in the Mediterranean countries. The use of alliteration (lots of Ws!!) helps British schoolchildren in geography lessons.

Chemistry students remember the following elements in this order:

Potassium (*kalium* in Latin)	K	Kittens
Sodium (*natrium* in Latin)	Na	Not
Calcium	Ca	Cats
Magnesium	Mg	Make
Aluminium	Al	A
Zinc	Zn	Zoo
Iron (*ferrum* in Latin)	Fe	For
Lead (*plumbum* in Latin)	Pb	Poor
Hydrogen	H	Hungry
Copper (*cuprum* in Latin)	Cu	Children

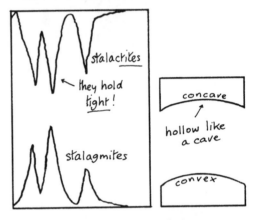

Children learning to play the piano must learn the notes of the treble clef. They remember the lines:

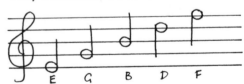

Every Good Boy Deserves Favour!

And the spaces:

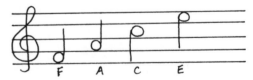

These are some of the ways of using poetry to help remember information. But what are the techniques for learning poetry? Do you just repeat and repeat until you get it right? Do you pace around the room repeating it? Do you try to get each line right before you go on to the next or do you try to learn a verse at a time? Do you think about the meaning or do you just concentrate on the sound of the words and the rhythm? Do you study the poetry just before you go to sleep or wake up early and learn it then?

The techniques described in this chapter on memory have emphasised the need to think about meaning. They have also referred to the usefulness of thinking of extremes (of extremely strange connections), of personal associations and of the quality of the language and imagery itself. Do you know of any other memory techniques not described in this chapter?

★★ Perhaps you and your class or friends could make a collection of all the memory techniques you know and make use of.

A good memory is undoubtedly a powerful tool. However, it is probably better to have a good memory for sources of information and the skill to use those sources than it is to remember a lot of detailed information. In the next chapter help is given to make the search for information easier and . . . faster.

Our memories are important to the police

The difference between 'memory' and 'remembering' is very important to the police. The police have to help people to remember without first putting the ideas and information into their minds. A great deal of police work is dependent on people's memories.

The police have various techniques for 'jogging' people's memories.

Photofit techniques are used: the witness is shown drawings of eyes, eyebrows, noses, mouths, ears, hair, etc. and asked to choose the ones which are similar to the person they saw. All these bits are put together until a face is made. Alternatively, the police might show the witness ten photographs of different people (including one photograph of someone the police suspect). The photograph might 'jog' the memory of the witness. Because the witness sees another nine photographs the police can say they didn't suggest which person the witness saw. (The photographs must be of people of similar appearance!) The same technique is used in an 'identity parade' in which the suspect is asked to stand in a line of ten other people of a similar appearance.

Some serious crimes are reconstructed, for example, the kidnapping of a child might be reconstructed. The police might use similar cars and people dressed up to act out what happened. Witnesses and the general public are shown this reconstruction and asked if they remember any different information. They might say, for example, 'the car had a radio aerial and had a long scratch down the side.' And this might be enough information for the police to find the car. The principle of this sort of memory jogging is that people can often remember if they see something very similar. It doesn't help if they are shown something which is totally different!

It is easy to think that a witness who saw a crime being committed will be able to give all the answers. However, witnesses are notoriously unreliable!

★ How good would you be as a witness? Continue to look down at this book and try to answer these questions:

– Can you describe, in detail, the appearance and clothing of the people around you?

– Can you describe, in detail, the objects in front of you?

★★ If you have a friend with you ask him or her to ask you questions about the people or the objects in front of you. Ask them to invent some things! For example, 'Is there a knife on the table?' You may find that your memory of the scene is better than you thought.

A picture history of memory

For thousands of years people have enjoyed rituals and ceremonies. In these ceremonies words and actions have been closely combined. The actions are probably easier to remember than words and help people remember what to say.

Did Simonides, the Greek poet, invent the next memory technique? He was once at a banquet reading his poetry. When he had finished he left the house and a few moments later the roof collapsed! Most of the other guests were killed. Simonides discovered that

he could remember where everybody had been sitting and was able to identify the bodies. He realised that he had found an idea for a marvellous memory technique, very valuable for a poet or storyteller (before there were any books)!

The great speakers in Roman and Greek times used this technique in order to remember their speeches. They thought of a place they knew well, for example, a temple, and then imagined the different parts of their speech connected to the doorway, to the first column, to a window, to a statue, etc. They imagined themselves walking around the building and then remembered their speech.

In the Middle Ages some systems for memorising were condemned by the church. The church thought that memory techniques were used by witches.

In Shakespeare's time the actors often used 'the place technique'. They thought of their own theatre.

In Cambridge in the 17th century, Henry Herdson invented another memory technique. He thought of objects which look like numbers. For example, he thought of a candle as one, a swan as two, etc. Then when he had to remember a list of ideas he connected them with each of the objects.

A priest called Reverend Brayshaw collected more than 2,000 dates and numerical facts from physics, history and geography and showed the unhappy schoolchildren of Victorian times how to remember them. The technique was more complicated than learning the facts like a parrot!

It is less important for us to remember facts today as we can find the information so easily in books and in computers. It is more important for us to remember *how* to find information than for us to remember it! Nevertheless a good memory can still be useful!

How to read faster . . . and understand more

How long does it take to learn to read faster?

If you read faster don't you understand less?

What are the techniques?

What is the evidence of success for these techniques?

By the end of this chapter I hope the answers to these questions will be clear.

What is the truth about faster reading?

What is fast reading?

According to Manya and Eric de Leeuw, the average speed of untrained people reading their own language is about 230 words per minute (w.p.m.). In their experiments the range went from 200 w.p.m. to over 400 w.p.m.

Michael Wallace says, 'I feel that all one can really say to a foreign learner is that, assuming medium-difficult material, a speed of less than 100 w.p.m. is very slow: it is doubtful whether students reading at this speed are grasping the essential meaning of medium-difficult texts. 100–200 w.p.m. is still slow. Any student within this range should be devoting some time to reading improvement. 200–300 w.p.m. is average, and a speed range at which fairly rapid improvement is possible. A speed of over 300 w.p.m. is very satisfactory.' If you would like to test your own reading speed turn to page 73 to see how to do so.

Training can increase reading speeds dramatically

Manya and Eric de Leeuw describe a group of ten psychiatrists who had an average reading speed of 334 w.p.m. before training. After training they had an average of 647 w.p.m. Reading speeds improved by 80–100% during a 30–40 hour course.

Comprehension increases!

The ten psychiatrists began with a 78% comprehension of the texts. At the end of the training, with their new reading speed, they had raised their comprehension to 85%. Speed reading usually increases comprehension because the reader concentrates on meanings given by the text as a whole rather than the variety of possible meanings of individual words.

Variation of speed

Of course you vary your reading speed according to the type of text and what you want to get out of it.

What is the speed reading record?

I don't know! However, speeds of 1,000 w.p.m. are possible. The eye can see up to six words in one glance, and it can move from one group of words to another four times every second.

Should we train the eye or the brain?

The eye can see at an amazing speed already. It is the brain which needs training. The eye passes on a lot of information and the brain must learn to select what is important. Art historians know what to look for in paintings in order to identify them, farmers know what to look for in animals in order to decide whether they are healthy or not. If the art historians and the farmers are experienced they know what to look for and can do it very quickly. It takes time to develop this ability.

Common faults in reading

Most people read more slowly than they need to. Slow readers (and students reading a text in a foreign language) usually read a text word by word. They want to make sure that they understand every word. And yet words by themselves can mean many things.

★ Look up a word in the dictionary and see how many meanings are given. What does the word 'work' mean? What does it mean in this sentence, 'He was told to improve his work efficiency'?

work (wɜːk) *n.* **1.** physical or mental effort directed towards doing or making something. **2.** paid employment at a job or a trade, occupation, or profession. **3.** a duty, task, or undertaking. **4.** something done, made, etc., as a result of effort or exertion: *a work of art*. **5.** materials or tasks on which to expend effort or exertion. **6.** another word for **workmanship** (sense 3). **7.** the place, office, etc., where a person is employed. **8.** any piece of material that is undergoing a manufacturing operation or process; workpiece. **9. a.** decoration or ornamentation, esp. of a specified kind. **b.** (in combination): *wirework; woolwork.* **10.** an engineering structure such as a bridge, building, etc. **11.** *Physics.* the transfer of energy expressed as the product of a force and the distance through which its point of application moves in the direction of the force. Abbrevs.: *W, w* **12.** a structure, wall, etc., built or used as part of a fortification system. **13. at work. a.** at one's job or place of employment. **b.** in action; operating. **14. make short work of.** *Informal.* to handle or dispose of very quickly. **15.** (*modifier*) of, relating to, or used for work: *work clothes; a work permit.* ~*vb.* **16.** (*intr.*) to exert effort in order to do, make, or perform something. **18.** (*tr.*) to carry on operations, activity, etc., in (a place or area): *that salesman works the southern region.* **19.** (*tr.*) to cause to labour or toil: *he works his men hard.* **20.** to operate or cause to operate, esp. properly or effectively: *to work a lathe; that clock doesn't work.* **21.** (*tr.*) to till or cultivate (land). **22.** to handle or manipulate or be handled or manipulated: *to work dough.* **23.** to shape, form, or process or be shaped, formed, or processed: *to work copper.* **24.** to reach or cause to reach a specific condition, esp. gradually: *the rope worked loose.* **25.** (*tr.*) *Chiefly U.S.* to solve (a mathematical problem). **26.** (*intr.*) to move in agitation: *his face worked with anger.* **27.** (*tr.*; often foll. by *up*) to provoke or arouse: *to work someone into a frenzy.* **28.** (*tr.*) to effect or accomplish: *to work one's revenge.* **29.** to make (one's way) with effort: *he worked his way through the crowd.* **30.** (*tr.*) to make or decorate by hand in embroidery, tapestry, etc.: *she was working a sampler.* **31.** (*intr.*) (of a mechanism) to move in a loose or otherwise imperfect fashion. **32.** (*intr.*) (of liquids) to ferment, as in brewing. **33.** (*tr.*) *Informal.* to manipulate or exploit to one's own advantage. **34.** (*tr.*) *Informal.* to cheat or swindle. ~See also **work back, work in, work off, work on, work out, work over, works, work up.** [Old English *weorc* (n.), *wircan, wyrcan* (vb.); related to Old High German *wurchen,* German *wirken,* Old Norse *yrkja,* Gothic *waurkjan*] —'**work·less** *adj.* —'**work·less·ness** *n.*

Meaning comes from whole phrases, sentences and paragraphs.

★★ Ask a friend to hold a book up and begin to read. Position yourself so that you can see his or her eyes. You will notice that the eyes move in small jerks and don't move smoothly along the lines of text. This is true of both slow readers and fast readers. The difference is that the slow reader looks at each word, keeps going back and sometimes looks away from the text altogether.

The faster reader also jumps but he

Most people read more slowly than they need to. Slow readers and

or she jumps longer distances! The faster reader sees groups of words rather than single words. Also he or she doesn't go back so often to read words

or phrases for a second or third time (although looking back to double check meaning is a very reasonable thing to do).

(Most people read)(more slowly)(than they)(need to.) (Slow readers)(and

★ Look at the sentence above. Look at the second word . . . 'people'. It is easy to see the words 'most' and 'read' on each side. Sometimes the words that fast readers see are simply close to each other, and sometimes the grouping is more to do with sense, for example, 'more slowly'.

Slow readers vocalise each word that they read. (They speak each word either out loud or to themselves.) If a person vocalises it is impossible for them to read faster than about 280 words per minute. Fast reading must be entirely silent and visual.

Some techniques and exercises for increasing your reading speed

1 The first technique is really an *attitude of mind*. If you want to read faster you will! Many people don't really want to. Everybody can walk faster than they normally do but they don't want to.

2 *Practice*. I can tell you many of the

established techniques for improving reading speeds. However, it isn't enough for you to know them. You must practise them over a period of several weeks.

3 *Seeing more words with each glance.* You can train yourself to do this. It is helpful to begin by analysing texts and dividing the sentences up into 'sense groups' of two to four words. Why not take paragraphs in this book? If possible actually mark the text with a pencil. If a friend is doing the same thing it is a good idea to use the same text and compare the way you have both divided it. There is no right and wrong in this exercise. However, it will give you a feeling of confidence and understanding of the process. Then take the same text and see how quickly you can read it. Do this with a number of texts during the first few days.

Don't restrict this exercise to the first day. (Remember that you learn more efficiently if you do a little bit over several days than a lot on one day.)

★ Try this. Open a book (use this one if you like). Hold your two forefingers out, parallel and about

DAYS

WPM	1	2	3	4	5	6	7	8	9	10	11	12	13	14	15	16	17	18	19	20	21	22	23	24	25	26	27	28	29	30
550																														
500																														
450																														
400																														
350																														
300																														
250																														
200																														
150																														
100																														

four words apart. Turn your eyes away and then let your fingers come down on the page. Try to see the three or four words between your fingers at a single glance. Do this repeatedly until your concentration goes.

★★ Work with a friend. Show him or her three or four words at a time for a very brief moment. Then cover the words and ask what they were.

These exercises help to change your attitude and approach to the number of words you expect to see at one glance.

4 *Use a pencil or ruler* or even your finger to direct your eyes and to give them a feeling of the speed you want to go. Move them along the lines quite quickly. This will both concentrate your attention and give you a sense of urgency.

5 *Begin by establishing your reading speed.* Take a text and read it for exactly three minutes. Work out your reading speed in the following way:

$$\text{W.P.M.} = \frac{\text{number of words you have read}}{\text{number of minutes you have spent}}$$

6 *Keep a record of your progress.* Here is a graph you can use. Use this graph for exercises from the same book or at least the same type of text. Try to spend at least 15 minutes each day on this practice.

7 *'Lightning speed' exercise.* Sometimes read four or five pages as fast as you can. Don't bother about comprehension. Then return to your normal speed. You should find that your normal speed is now 50–100 w.p.m. faster!

If you would like to follow a course in speed reading, I recommend you look at:

Edward Fry: *Reading Faster*, Cambridge University Press (Elementary)

Gerald and Vivienne Mosback: *Practical Faster Reading*, Cambridge University Press (Upper-intermediate/Advanced)

Manya and Eric de Leeuw: *Read Better, Read Faster*, Pelican

How to improve your reading efficiency

In the previous section I described some of the ways of increasing the speed of your reading. In this section I shall concentrate on ways of improving the comprehension of texts.

Try this text. See how well you understand the main ideas in the text and remember some of the main examples. Read as quickly as you can and time yourself. Work out your w.p.m. (There are 578 words in the text.)

Gesture

Although we are not normally aware of it, most of us use our hands when we are talking. You can see this by turning down the sound on your television set. Notice how much the speakers use their hands as they talk. Our hands can show the shape and size of things (try describing a spiral staircase without using your hands!) and *emphasise* what we are saying. Some gestures, though, have special meanings; what do these people seem to be saying?

These gestures are not made naturally: we have to learn them and they vary from one country to another. For example, how do you call someone to you? In Spain and many other countries you *beckon* someone with your palm *down*, which can look like the English sign for sending someone away. In Italy you wave goodbye with the *back* of your hand which can look like the English sign for beckoning someone!

What do you mean when you nod or shake your head? Nodding seems to be one of the few gestures found in nearly every country; it seems to mean 'yes' almost everywhere but in some parts of India, for example, *shaking* the head *also* means 'yes'. In Greece and Southern Italy and many other parts of the world, throwing the head back, which can look like a nod, means 'no'.

When you see your friends, how do you greet them? People in many countries find the English cold and unfriendly because they often do no more than say 'hello'. Even adults shake hands usually only the first time they meet. French people, including schoolchildren, shake hands with their friends, or kiss them on both cheeks if they are close friends, each time they meet and when they leave one another. At home they do not go to bed without kissing everyone in the family good night, on both cheeks, and shaking hands with any visitors. The same thing happens in the morning. How do you think a French child might feel staying in your family?

Other countries have different ways of greeting. The Eskimos rub noses. In Samoa people sniff one another and in Polynesia you take hold of your friend's hands and use them to stroke your face. In Tibet it is very polite to stick your tongue out at someone; you are saying 'there is no evil thought on my tongue'!

In some parts of East Africa it is considered very unlucky to point with your fingers and so people turn their heads and pout their lips in the direction they mean. In Britain some people 'cross their fingers' for good luck but in Austria and Germany they hold their thumbs. In Britain, if the people in an audience do not like a performer and if they are not very polite they may clap their hands slowly to mean 'go away!'. In other parts of Europe the slow hand clap is a great compliment! In Britain people may stand up as a sign of respect. In some other countries they sit down to show that they look *up* to the person.

There are many other signs used in different countries, and what is an insult in one country may not be understood or may have quite a different meaning in another. The English do not use gesture as much as many other people and it is very easy for misunderstandings to arise.

Test your comprehension. How much have you understood? Don't look at the text again, but try to remember what you have read.
1 What is the author's main point?
2 Can you think of any other general points?
3 How many examples can you think of for each point?
4 What does the author want the young British reader to do as a result of reading this text?
When you have written down everything you remember, look at the text again. Check your answers.

The following techniques should help you to improve your comprehension without reducing your speed. There is one thing in common to all the techniques described here: the reader must be active. The reader should have a need, a purpose, an interest or a point of view when reading a text.

Anticipation

In many situations we can anticipate what another person is going to say or do. We may think of various alternatives, of course, and not just one thing, and this allows us to respond quickly. But sometimes we don't prepare ourselves (or the other person may do something quite unexpected). Then we need time to think about it if we are to make a sensible response. A common example of when we need to anticipate, and avoid disaster when the other person does the unexpected, is in driving!

Writing is another way in which people can speak to us, and we can (and do) use the technique of anticipation when we read. It helps us to respond quickly. (However, there is a danger: if we anticipate wrongly we may not really concentrate on what the other person is telling us; we assume we know what the other person is saying. Arrogant anticipation can make us blind to new ideas and to originality.)

When we drive or when we meet people we anticipate by getting

information from people's appearance and behaviour and from the nature of the place where they are . . . and this may include something which we see or hear. When we pick up a book or a magazine we anticipate the content and the character of the text by the design of the cover, the quality of the paper and the printing, and, of course, by the title, the author's name and the publisher.

If the subject or the author is familiar to us then we will probably have opinions, questions, and needs related to it. It is astonishing, however, that we can often guess at some of the content of texts which might seem quite strange to us at first. Look at the books opposite and try to guess what the texts might be about.

Your ability to guess at the content of the book will be determined by:

1 Your understanding of the language.
2 Your understanding of the visual design, i.e. the choice of typeface and the shapes the designer has chosen.

For example, for a British reader, the style of the type chosen for *The Tale of Timmy Tiptoes* is old and charming. And that fits in well with the charming picture (for a British reader!) of a squirrel wearing a jacket!

The typeface chosen for *Modern Quotations* is modern, direct and bold. However, some of the text on the cover is italic and implies old-fashioned qualities of style and class. The quotation, ' "Carry on Cohens, we need you " – The Times' is in the style of type used in newspapers. The designer has made the cover of the book appear to be informal and varied.

Through our response to the words and the design we begin to anticipate what we shall find when we open the book.

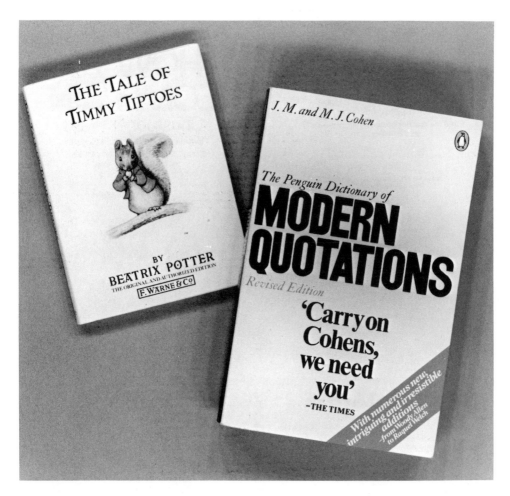

Surveying

When you are walking in the countryside you might stop on a hill top and 'survey' the countryside. You can look at its general character before you look at the individual bits. It is wise to survey information books in the same way.

SURVEYING THE CONTENTS, ETC.

You can get an idea of the nature of the book from:
– The publisher's blurb on the back of the book, in which the publisher describes the book in a few words.
– The contents page which lists the titles of the chapters.
– The preface or introduction, in which the author makes some general comments about the book.

★ Imagine. You are going on a long train journey and you want to buy a book. You go into the station bookshop, but you only have two or three minutes to choose a book, so you quickly look at two books. On the next page are the covers of the books. Which would you choose?

How to complain
and
How to get results from

**RESTAURANTS • COMPANIES
LANDLORDS • BRITISH RAIL
THE GAS BOARD • AIRLINES
GARAGES • TAX INSPECTORS
HOLIDAY OPERATORS • BANKS
SHOPS • THE ELECTRICITY BOARD**
and most other causes of aggravation
and exasperation

A consumer's handbook with all the short cuts
and lists of those who can help you
win your battles

'Gives a lot of sound advice, laced with
quite a few laughs'
KATIE BOYLE **TV TIMES**

REFERENCE INFORMATION
0 330 25947 4

HOW TO COMPLAIN Christopher Ward

HOW TO COMPLAIN
Christopher Ward
"Practical, sensible, meticulously
accurate and delightfully vicious"
BERNARD LEVIN, THE TIMES

Bang up to date for the 80's
ILLUSTRATED

FOOL'S PARADISE

explains who gets rich from the tourist industry
and how they do it.

It's all here from the travel agent's rake-off to the
souvenir seller's split of the pickings.

Everything the tourist eats, drinks, buys or takes
home makes somebody rich – and here's how it
works . . . fast food frauds and restaurant rip-offs,
credit card and traveller's cheque rackets, the
hotel as round-the-clock money machine, package
tour profiteers and long-distance coach rides that
are just a dice game with death . . .

The author of the bestselling
AIRPORT INTERNATIONAL*
takes a long hard look at the tourist industry
worldwide. Read it and you may never go on
holiday again. If you do, at least you'll know the
tricks of the trade.

A PAN ORIGINAL

*also available in Pan.

TRAVEL/CONSUMER AFFAIRS
0 330 26240 8

FOOL'S PARADISE BRIAN MOYNAHAN

SURVEYING THE CHAPTERS

If you think you have found a useful book you should survey the general sense of the chapters. One way of doing this is to read the first and the last paragraphs of a chapter. The aim of the chapter may be in the first paragraph and the summary of the points made may be in the last paragraph. You should be able to judge the style of the author. Do you like it? Here are the first and last paragraphs of the chapter on Advertisements in *How to Complain*.

First paragraph:

Hard though it is to believe, there is a rule that all advertisements must be 'legal, decent, honest and truthful'.

Last paragraph:

What about classified ads? Deals between private individuals are not protected by the law, so beware of the small-ad seller who offers you a parrot with a vocabulary of two thousand words.

Here are the first and last paragraphs from the Introduction to *Fool's Paradise*.

First paragraph:

It will not seem it to the man at Luton Airport with the bucket and spade and the children and the delayed departure to the Spanish sun, but he is the core of an industry of phenomenal growth that is expected to be second only to defence by the end of the century. Tourism already employs more than world oil and steel combined, though based simply on the 'four Ss', Sun, Sand, Sea and Sex.

Last paragraph:

Even the basics, eating, drinking and sleeping, turn out to be far from simple on careful examination.

When you have a good sense of the book after surveying the chapters you can decide which of the books to buy. (In the case of these two examples I bought both of them!)

Scanning

Imagine that you have surveyed the countryside and that you have a general idea of it. Now you decide that you would like to walk through it and you want to plan your route. You must, therefore, look at certain details of the route. Is there a river? Where can you cross it? Is there an area of private ground? In the same way, you might scan a contents list of a book for one particular subject. You only 'have eyes for' that subject.

★ Imagine. The cost of heating your house during the last three months has been enormous! You have tried to find out if there has been some mistake, but you never receive replies to your letters. How do you complain? Overleaf is the first page of the contents list of *How to Complain*. Scan it quickly. Which of the people or institutions would you like to complain to?

The organisation of the text

If you understand how the text is organised then you can find the information more quickly. (If you understand how a library is organised then you can find the book you want faster than someone who walks up and down every shelf until finding it at last!)

In the majority of informational texts the first sentence contains the main idea of the paragraph. If the first sentence doesn't contain the main idea then the last sentence may do. Here are some basic ways of structuring a text;

CONTENTS

the first four would usually be for informational texts and the fifth for fiction.

1 In scientific texts it is very common to begin by stating a problem and then go on to describe an idea about the problem. Following this, experiments are described and finally conclusions are given.

2 Some descriptions of events are described in the order in which they happened.

3 Some descriptions of events emphasise cause and effect.

4 Some descriptions give a broad summary before giving details and examples.

5 More literary or entertaining texts may begin with a detail and not state any general conclusions.

★ Here are six texts. Read them and decide what kind of structure has been used in each text.

Councillor in crash

Didsbury Councillor Harold Steel, a former Lord Mayor, has been injured in a car crash in South Manchester. The Councillor, due for re-election next June, was in a multiple car pile-up in Northendon last Sunday afternoon. He is now in bed at home with a broken arm but thinks he will be able to fight the next election. 'I'm pretty tough,' said Councillor Steel. 'I'll be back on my feet within a couple of days.'
(Based on newspaper article)

Proper custard sauce

. . . First heat the cream in a small saucepan up to boiling point; and while it's heating thoroughly blend the egg yolks, cornflour, sugar and vanilla together in a small basin. Then pour the hot cream in – stirring all the time – and return the mixture to the saucepan. Heat very gently (still stirring) until the sauce has thickened, which should only take a minute or two.
(Delia Smith, *Complete Cookery Course*)

Katy growing up

'Can I get changed while you aren't here please?' she said.
'Are you serious?'
'Not really. I don't mean it!' And she pushed me out of the door, her little finger ends pressed against my back.
Yesterday I found a note:
DEAR SEAN
I LOVE YOU. DO YOU LOVE ME?
(Andrew Wright, *Moments*)

Damp in buildings

Dampness can lead to decay in a building: wallpaper peels from the walls, wood rots and fungus grows on the walls. The building may be ruined and the people who live and work in it may become unhealthy.

Dampness in buildings is often caused by humidity. Sometimes the air contains a lot of moisture; if the air then meets a cold wall or other cold surface it cools and deposits some of the moisture on the surfaces. If you want to find out whether dampness in your home is caused by con-densation rather than by any other cause you might like to try out this experiment.

Fix a small piece of glass against a wall in your home. (You can fix it with an adhesive but make sure there is a small gap between the glass and the wall.) After a day, examine the glass: if there is moisture on the room side of the glass the dampness is caused by condensation. If the dampness is beneath the glass then the moisture is coming through the wall from the outside.

In order to reduce humidity in your house you should make sure that moisture caused by cooking does not spread through the house. For example, fix an air extractor to the window in your kitchen . . .
(Based on a manufacturer's leaflet)

The man who lost his wife

It was unusually cold the day I lost my wife. The windows cleared as we set off but the visibility wasn't too good. When I saw that we were low on petrol I stopped at a petrol station. My wife said she would clean the windows. She cleaned the front ones lifting the wipers quite carefully. Then she went round to the back of the car and I never saw her again. When she didn't come back I thought she must have gone to the toilets. But after some time when she didn't come back I got out and asked the attendant if he had seen her go into the toilets. Then I asked a woman to go in to see if she was there. She wasn't. The attendant didn't even seem to remember her getting out of the car. I phoned the police but they never found her.
(Andrew Wright, *Moments*)

Learning to read

Some children develop their awareness of language and their ability to use it at an early age. And some find little problem in learning to read. Although children have different natural propensities to use language a key influence in their success (or their lack of success) is the amount of time that adults listen to them and talk to them.
(Based on research into the development of children's reading)

If you would like to compare your analyses of these six texts with mine, turn to page 85. Please note that analyses of this kind aren't right or wrong but are personal interpretations.

Summary of reading techniques and skills for informational texts

1 Be active. Use a book in the same way that you would use a library.
2 Survey the contents page, chapters, etc.
3 Try to anticipate what the book offers and what you want from it.
4 Try to find out how the texts are organised.
5 Either read (with your new speed reading) all the texts or scan the texts for the particular information you need to know.
BUT!

Some objections to these techniques

Here are six objections produced by a group of students when they discussed the points in this section. Would you agree with them? Would you add any other objections?

1 'Surely most of these techniques only apply to information books?'
2 'I don't want to anticipate when I'm reading a story. I like to be surprised and carried along by the writer.'
3 'I often like to daydream when I'm reading a text, even an information text, then I begin to invent my own ideas. I can't do this if I'm rushing along trying to think of the fastest way of getting information.'
4 'I might be able to get the content of the text better and faster with these techniques, but I don't think I can enjoy the style and the poetry of the language in these ways.'
5 'Sometimes you know what you want and sometimes you might have a good point of view of your own. But when you read you can get totally new ideas and ways of thinking if you are open to them. And I think these techniques must be used very carefully. They can be dangerous if they close your mind to new ideas.'
6 'Some really great writers may seem to be using a common type of organisation but are not. And it is this twist of what is old into something new which is their power. If you think you can predict their type of organisation you can miss a lot.'

The points of view expressed above are serious and show that reading quickly is not always the most appropriate way to find some kinds of information. Sometimes it is satisfying and rewarding to wander slowly through a beautiful or interesting place. However, sometimes it is very useful to be able to run!

Last thoughts

Our brain is a wonderful possession. Do we use it as well as we might? Do we think as we have always thought? In this book I have described a few ideas which I hope you have found useful. Physical work makes the muscles strong and mental work makes the mind strong. Very often, mental work means learning what other people have said and done. And in traditional, formal, education, if you do something it is often a copy of what someone else has done. In this book the emphasis is on what *you* do and on what strengths you find yourself.

Doing is important; looking at a lot of information, developing opinions and ideas about it, sorting it out, arranging it into groups, writing about it and sharing it with other people. That is what I have tried to do in this book. If you have found it one tenth as useful to read it as I have to write it, then it may have been of some value to you! I hope so.

Answers

Page 12

Alex and Brian say different things about Chris. Therefore, one of them is lying and Chris must be telling the truth. Since Chris says he was before Alex, it is obvious that Alex is lying about coming first. Therefore the real order must have been: Brian (who wasn't second, according to Chris who told the truth), then Chris (because Brian said so, and he also was telling the truth) – finally Alex.

Page 12

The answer demonstrates the need for visual thinking. The new door would have to be at 5.

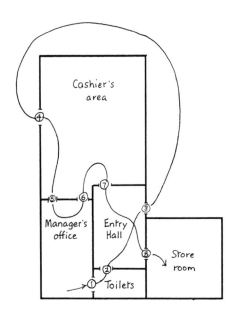

Page 13

Possibility 1

1st year: 2,000 + 2,000 = 4,000
2nd year: 2,025 + 2,025 = 4,050
3rd year: 2,050 + 2,050 = 4,100
4th year: 2,075 + 2,075 = 4,150
5th year: 2,100 + 2,100 = 4,200

Possibility 2

1st year: 2,000 + 2,020 = 4,020
2nd year: 2,040 + 2,060 = 4,100
3rd year: 2,080 + 2,100 = 4,180
4th year: 2,120 + 2,140 = 4,260
5th year: 2,160 + 2,180 = 4,340

Page 15

This is one possible solution:

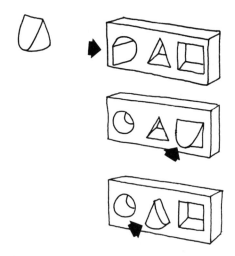

Page 15

The first die in the third pair.

Page 21

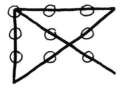

The problem didn't say that you couldn't go beyond the dots. You thought the problem meant that you couldn't go beyond the dots.

Can you find more answers? Stand back from the problem! A ten-year-old child gave the following answer:

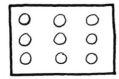

Page 27

At the moment the tutor is behaving like a cat. He is playing with the student, he lets the student say something and then easily proves that what the student says is foolish. The student is acting like a mouse because he is willing to respond to the questions and thus gets caught again and again. The student could think about the cat and mouse analogy and decide to behave like a hedgehog instead.

He could become 'prickly' and difficult. He could 'roll into a ball' and refuse to answer some of the questions. He could avoid answering some

questions and reply aggressively and only take one part of the question. This would make the game of being a 'cat' less amusing for the tutor. Or the student could become a hedgehog that just carries on walking in the direction he wants to go in. The student would answer some questions but not all and would do so in a fairly 'prickly' way.

Above all the student should realise that the tutor is playing a cat and mouse game. This realisation will, at least, make the student into a 'wary mouse' so that he is not caught so easily in the first place. He will learn how to avoid open places where he can get caught and will learn how to get to places by different, safer routes.

Page 43

There are various possible headings, for example:
1 Many West Indian families
2 Children don't look at the teacher
3 Some teachers only want to teach reading/writing/arithmetic
4 Alternative subjects to teach, social skills, etc.
5 Poor building and shortage of equipment.

Page 53

'To hit something with the foot' = kick
'To plunge head first into water' = dive
'To exchange something for money' = sell

Page 81

Councillor in crash – Text structure 4
Proper custard sauce – Text structure 2
Katy growing up – Text structure 5
Damp in buildings – Text structure 1
The man who lost his wife – Text structure 4
Learning to read – Text structure 1

Acknowledgements

The author and publishers are grateful to the following authors, publishers and others who have given permission for the use of copyright material identified in the text. It has not been possible to identify the sources of all the material used and in such cases the publishers would welcome information from copyright owners.

Archivi Alinari for the 'Self-Portrait' by Leonardo da Vinci on p. 8, from Turin Library; Windsor Castle Royal Library for the anatomical study by Leonardo on p. 9, copyright reserved, reproduced by gracious permission of Her Majesty the Queen; the Trustees of the British Museum for Leonardo's machines on p. 9; BBC Hulton Picture Library for the photograph of Einstein on p. 10; The Metropolitan Museum of Art, New York, for 'Angel of Revelation' by William Blake, 1757–1827, on p. 18 (watercolour with pen and ink); Collins Publishers for the extracts on pp. 27 and 71 from the *Collins English Dictionary*; Longman Group Ltd for the extract on p. 28 from the *Longman Dictionary of English Idioms*; the Board of the British Library for the woodcut on p. 64, dated 1490; Penguin Books Ltd for the extract on p. 64 from *The Knight's Tale* from Geoffrey Chaucer *The Canterbury Tales*, translated by Neville Coghill (Penguin Classics 1951, reprinted with revisions 1958, 1960, 1975, 1977), copyright © 1951 by Neville Coghill, 1958, 1969, 1975, 1977, for the jacket illustration on p. 74 from *The Tale of Timmy Tiptoes* by Beatrix Potter (Frederick Warne, 1911) copyright © 1911 Frederick Warne, London, and for the jacket illustration on p. 74 from *The Penguin Dictionary of Modern Quotations* by J.M. Cohen and M.J. Cohen (Penguin Reference Books, 1971, second edition 1980); Manchester Public Libraries for the extract from the Ellesmere Chaucer on p. 65; Helen Astley for the extract from *Get the Message* on pp. 74–5; Pan Books Ltd for the covers on p. 78 of *How to Complain* by Christopher Ward and *Fool's Paradise* by Brian Moynahan; Martin Secker and Warburg Ltd for the extracts on pp. 79–80 from *How to Complain* by Christopher Ward; A.D. Peters and Co Ltd for the extracts on p. 79 from *Fool's Paradise* by Brian Moynahan; BBC Publications for the extract on p. 81 from Delia Smith's *Complete Cookery Course*; Pilgrims Publications for the extracts on p. 81 from *Moments* by Andrew Wright.